𝕮𝖔𝖑𝖚𝖒𝖇𝖎𝖆 𝖀𝖓𝖎𝖛𝖊𝖗𝖘𝖎𝖙𝖞

STUDIES IN ENGLISH AND COMPARATIVE LITERATURE

FROISSART

AND THE

ENGLISH CHRONICLE PLAY

"The Epic may wither and the Tragedy fail, but there is seldom want of the good bread of chronicles . . . and there is as little weariness in them as in any things composed by men."

W. P. KER.

FROISSART

AND THE

ENGLISH CHRONICLE PLAY

BY

ROBERT METCALF SMITH, Ph.D.

SOMETIME UNIVERSITY SCHOLAR AND UNIVERSITY FELLOW IN ENGLISH,
COLUMBIA UNIVERSITY

Benjamin Blom

First published 1915 by Columbia University Press
Reissued 1965 by Benjamin Blom, Inc., Bronx 10452
L.C. Catalog Card No.: 65-16250

Printed in U.S.A. by
NOBLE OFFSET PRINTERS, INC.
NEW YORK 3, N. Y.

PREFACE

The present study was undertaken in order to disclose the relationship existing between the *Chronicles* of John Froissart and historical literature in England up to the seventeenth century when the Tudor Chronicle plays vanished from the stage. During the last two decades, critical scholarship has discovered many intimate relations between French and English lyric and romance of the medieval period, and between the writings of the Pléiade and the poetry of the Elizabethan age. Investigation, however, of Froissart's connections with English Literature has been almost wholly confined to his poetry, chiefly with reference to that of his friend, Geoffrey Chaucer. Froissart's most noted work, the *Chronicles*, which was translated into English by Lord Berners as early as 1523–5, has been generally overlooked as a source for the sixteenth century chroniclers, and the succeeding dramatists of English history. Moreover, in searching for sources of chronicle history plays, critics have confined their attention too exclusively to the *Chronicles* of Holinshed, largely perhaps, because Shakespeare has given this history such enviable prestige. But other and better chronicles of this period also found eager readers. Today, when any question arises concerning sources for chronicle plays, the easy and immediate answer is Holinshed. In opposition, then, to what might become a facile dogmatism, the following pages endeavor to reveal to what extent those chapters in Froissart's *Chronicles* that relate English history, particularly the reigns of Edward III and Richard II, influenced the chroniclers and playwrights of the Elizabethan age.

To facilitate this investigation, the first two chapters
review the life and literary work of Froissart, and of his
translator, Lord Berners. In writing these chapters I have
availed myself freely of the excellent work of previous in-
vestigators, and have, therefore, presented little that is
original. The remainder of the first part discloses the
continuous vogue of Berners' *Froissart* among the long
succession of English Chroniclers; and demonstrates in
nearly every case their literal indebtedness to this translation. The second part discusses in detail the numerous
poetic and dramatic versions of Edward III and Richard
II in Elizabethen literature, and attempts to prove the
indebtedness of the authors to Berners' translation. Chapter IV presents the new and complete sources from Berners for the anonymous play *Edward III*, wrongly supposed to be derived from Holinshed, and reviews in this
light the question of authorship. Chapters VI and VII
offer for the plays, *Jack Straw* and *Woodstock* sources that
heretofore have been either incorrectly, or partially traced.
The last two chapters show the use made of Berners by
Samuel Daniel while writing the *Civil Wars*, and, in view
of this relationship, throw new light on the indebtedness
of Shakespeare's *Richard II* to Daniel's epic.

It gives me pleasure to acknowledge my gratitude to
all who have aided me in the course of this study. Among
those deserving special mention is Professor George B.
Churchill of Amherst College, to whose masterly teaching
I am personally indebted, and whose authoritative monograph on Richard III has given me very material assistance
in chapter III. From the members of the Department of
English and Comparative Literature of Columbia University I have received generous assistance. Professors W.
W. Lawrence, H. M. Ayres and G. P. Krapp have kindly
read and criticized the manuscript during its formation.

Most of all am I grateful to Professor A. H. Thorndike, who has had charge of the thesis from its inception, and who has unfailingly proffered invaluable criticism. Through the kindness of the Journal of English and Germanic Philology, I am able to reprint portions of my chapter on Edward III, which appeared in January, 1911.

R. M. S.

March, 1915.

TO MY MOTHER

CONTENTS

PART I

FROISSART IN ENGLAND BEFORE THE CHRONICLE PLAY

CHRONOLOGICAL OUTLINE FOR CHAPTER I

1327 Accession of Edward the Third.

1337–8? Birth of Jean Froissart.

1341 War between England and Scotland. King Edward and the Countess of Salisbury.

1346 Battle of Crecy.

1347 Capture of Calais.

1356 Battle of Poitiers.

1361 Froissart in England at Queen Philippa's court.

1367 Froissart with the Black Prince at Bordeaux.

1368 Froissart with Chaucer in the wedding suite of Lionel, Duke of Clarence.

1370 Froissart under the patronage of Robert de Namur.

1372 Froissart appointed Cure de Lestinnes.

1376 Death of the Black Prince.

1377 Accession of Richard II.

1378 First Book of *Chronicles* extended to 1377.

1383 Froissart under patronage of Guy de Blois. Redaction of First Book of *Chronicles*.

1387 Second Book of *Chronicles* (1376–1386).

1390 Third Book of *Chronicles* (1386–1389).

1391 Froissart leaves Guy de Blois.

1394 Froissart visits England.

1399 Murder of Richard II.

1400 Fourth Book of *Chronicles* (1389–1400).

1400–1410 Last Redaction of First Book of *Chronicles*.

1410? Death of Froissart.

CHAPTER I

FROISSART AND HIS CHRONICLES

The *Chronicles* of Froissart have never wanted the reverence and honor generously accorded to works that are not for an age but for all time; and many English writers have acknowledged the inspiration received from the pen of this zealous chronicler of the Middle Ages. Thomas Gray hailed him as "the Herodotus of a barbarous age," and Scott, who frequently adopted the style of the old historian, warmly expressed his devotion in the words of Claverhouse in *Old Mortality*, saying that the pleasure of reading Froissart would repay for six months imprisonment. "His chapters inspire me with more enthusiasm than even poetry itself, and the noble canon, with what true chivalrous feeling, he confines his beautiful expressions of sorrow to the death of the gallant and high-bred knight of whom it was a pity to see the fall, and such was his loyalty to his king, pure faith to his religion, hardihood towards his enemy, and fidelity to his lady-love! Ah, benedicite! how he will mourn over the fall of such a pearl of knighthood, be it on the side he happen to favor or on the other! But truly for sweeping from the face of the earth some few hundred of villain churls, who are born but to plow it, the high born and inquisitive historian has marvellous little sympathy."

The life of Froissart has been so well written by Madame Darmsteter following the monumental researches of Kervyn de Lettenhove and of Siméon Luce, that no attempt has been made in the present review to add anything new; but

3

as an introduction to the following discussions, it has seemed best to retrace briefly the events of the chronicler's life, with special attention to his relations with the English court. He was born at Valenciennes in Hainault, but the year of his birth is still uncertain. Froissart, our only authority, makes several allusions to his age in his poetry and chronicles, not entirely consistent with one another. In the *Joli Buisson de Jeunesse*, he says he was thirty-five years old on November 30, 1373; accordingly he was born in 1338. But this date is contradicted by one passage in the chronicles, "Sachez que l'an de grâce 1390, j'avais cinquante-sept ans"—a statement which would establish the date 1333; several other passages however lead to the conclusion that he was born most probably in the winter of 1337.

Valenciennes was then a prosperous town in the Belgian province of Hainault, about twenty miles from the present Franco-Belgian border. The trade of Valenciennes with London had developed so rapidly that in 1340 the town must have seemed a "grand ville" to the surrounding villagers, and undoubtedly attracted large numbers of artisans and merchants to settle there and share its prosperity. Kervyn de Lettenhove suggests that the father of Froissart was one of these. But of his family and teachers Froissart says not a word in all his immense work. Some scholars, on the evidence of one of his pastorals, have attributed to his father the first name Thomas, and the profession of armorial painter. On the other hand, one might conclude from the *Joli Buisson de Jeunesse* that his father was a merchant of woolens. One ingenious biographer says that the boy was a natural child brought up by a disagreeable tutor, for at the age of twenty-one Froissart uttered no regrets on leaving his native province.

As a youngster his eager, inquisitive mind gave promise

of his wandering and varied life. His poem *l'Espinette Amoureuse* mingles a delightfully literal account of the youthful days which he spent in Valenciennes, hating his Latin and loving "les belles filles," with the traditional forms of allegorical love-making of chivalric France. He tells us he disliked games like chess that made him sit down and think, but he gives us a list of fifty-two that he did enjoy, half of which are unknown to the child of France today. He loved to chase the butterfly and to fly feathers against the wind. From the time he was twelve, he filled his mind with hunting, dancing, feasts, wine, dress, and women,—tastes which never left him. We are not surprised to find, therefore, that his ennui over his Latin exceeded even that over chess, especially when on the same bench with him at school were charming little girls to whom he made love by gifts of apples and pears, and who made him cry:

> " Quand donc viendra le temps pour moi
> Que par amours pourrai aimer? "

This susceptibility led him into a love affair that continued from his fourteenth to his twentieth year, and formed the subject matter for the love story in *l'Espinette Amoureuse*, one of the most entertaining poems of the fourteenth century. It would be difficult as well as useless to try to determine how much of what he narrates is fact, and how much is pure imagination. Certainly life at Valenciennes filled him with the spirit of romance and chivalry. In fashionable allegory, he describes with charming detail this beautiful young lady who set his fifteen year old heart aflame. She walked one day at a garden party with him at her side. She stooped to pluck five violets and gave him three, while she treasured the others. Then she begged him to lend her a romance. After many fears lest he be unable to fulfil her wish, he succeeded in obtaining an old copy of *Bailli d'Amour* and in return she lent him the romance of *Cleomadès*. But when his suit seemed progressing most hopefully, Froissart suddenly discovered himself totally out of favor because an enemy had whispered a calumny. He says that the lady seized him by the hair and pulled out a handful, then married another, whereupon overcome with grief he relieved his despair in a new ballade.

We may only imagine how Froissart, the amorous young poet and gallant of Hainault, sailed to England in 1361 to present to Queen Philippa his first essay in history, describing the latest exploits of the English. Mme. Darmsteter suggests that Jean le Bel, who finished his chronicle in the very year that Froissart began writing history, had recognized in the young poet a worthy successor, and accordingly financed his journey. Of this rhyming history Froissart wrote: "Howbeit I took on me, as soon as I came from school, to write and recite the said book and bare the same compiled into England and presented the volume thereof to my lady Philippa of Hainault, noble Queen of England, who right amiably received it to my great profit and advancement." This book now non-extant, but probably couched in the ordinary verse of romance, testified to Froissart's historical interest and his ability to take notes, as well as to write poetry. At first he did not think kindly of writing in prose, since no gentleman of that day considered prose fit to read. But after he had decided to carry on the history of Jean le Bel, he abandoned verse for prose, and correcting his previous efforts, set about honoring the great deeds of heroes in earnest.

For the next eight years (1361–1369) Froissart lived at the court of Edward III as poet and secretary for the Queen, who encouraged him to compose at length a history of the wars between France and England. As a guide and basis for material on the first years of the war (1325–1356) he adapted the chronicles of Jean le Bel, which he completed and verified. Garrulous old cavaliers and heralds who had witnessed the accession of Edward III, the first campaign against the Scots, and the declaration of war against France, furnished more stories for Froissart's eager ears and pen. In 1365, Queen Philippa sent him into Brittany and Lombardy to learn about the French-English wars in these provinces, and also into Scotland that he might journey for three months from village to village under the guidance of Bruce, King of the Scots, become acquainted with those northern knights who had witnessed the early conquests of Edward III, and see the castle at Berkeley where Edward II suffered his horrible death. Quite likely Froissart was already at the redaction of his first efforts, when in the middle of the year 1366, as war was breaking out in Castile, the Queen summoned him to accompany the Black Prince, to France. On the sixth of January, 1367, he writes: "I was in the cytie of Burdeaux, and sittyng at the table whare Kyng Richarde was borne the which was on a tuisday about X of the clock."[1] Toward the middle of February, the Black Prince sent him back to England with a message for the Queen.

One must remember, however, that it was in the office of poet, and not historian, that Froissart became famous during the eight years that he was attached to Queen Philippa, "le servant," as he says, "de beaux dittiés et de traités amoureux" in verse. Doubtless it was in this capacity that early in the following year, 1368, he was sent to Italy in the wedding train of Lionel, Duke of Clarence. Here he was much gratified to hear one of his virelais sung at the court of Savoy during the grand fête offered to the Duke of Clarence.

[1] Berners' Translation, London, 1812.

But in August, 1369, Froissart learned of the death of his patroness, Queen Philippa, and realized that his hopes were ruined. "Elle me fit et crea" he tells us. In losing her, he lost everything. At the court of Edward III the great reaction against Queen Philippa and her little court of Hainuyers, drove Froissart to seek refuge in Hainault. But his old friends took little interest in him and failed to foster his sensitive genius. After a year of grief over his loss, his consequent neglect, and his discomfort from the inconsistencies between his temperament and the situations in which he was placed, Froissart sought the relatives of his former patroness, and attached himself in 1370, first to Duke Wenceslas and then to Robert of Namur, the brilliant nephew of Queen Philippa, and a fairly constant supporter of the English, who not only served as a patron, but furnished Froissart with some of his own valuable documents. In September, 1373, Froissart was provided with the curacy of Lestinnes in Hainault, where he remained ten years, devoting most of his time to his chronicles and incidentally drinking a good deal of Flemish wine, baptising infants, and burying the dead. In 1378, he concluded and dedicated to Robert of Namur the first compilation of his chronicles, which covers the years 1325–1377. This first version, begun under the favor of Queen Philippa, and continued under Robert of Namur, naturally displays the glory of the English conquerors and shows strong English sympathies. Of this version many manuscripts are still extant, some of them illuminated with rare elaboration.

But by 1383 Froissart had become the chaplain of a new patron, Gui de Blois, whose ancestors had fought for France at Crecy. Froissart, newly appointed canon of Chimay, now changed his opinion rather than take the consequences of trying to sail his feather against the wind, for his new patrons and friends were strong sympathizers with the French. He therefore finished before 1383 a redaction of the chronicles, revised to harmonize with the French point of view; yet in this, as in his other revisions, he never excelled the fire and strength, the brilliance and picturesqueness of the original, and never again did he write with such devotion to the English cause. In comparison with the original this redaction is colorless and restrained, full of inserted references to the valiant cavaliers of the Blois family. Doubtless they were pleased, but others regretted that the fire and movement of the original were subdued to suit the peaceful atmosphere of the French presbyteries.

As critics have often noted, it is more than probable that Froissart was acquainted personally with Chaucer, since both looked to Queen Philippa for patronage, and both served in the train of Lionel, Duke of Clarence. It is not strange, therefore, that there are several similar passages in their works, and that there is a nice question to be decided by scholars as to which poet was the borrower. Professor Kittredge in his discussion of the date of the *Méliador,* Froissart's "fluent and interminable Arthurian romance," offers sufficient evidence to prove that Froissart's early version of *Paradys d'Amours* must have been written several years before 1369, the date of Chaucer's *Book of the Duchess,* and that Chaucer is, therefore, the imitator of Froissart's *Paradys d'Amours.*[1] Recently, Professor Lowes, by examining "parallel groupings of well known conventions which occur in other combinations elsewhere and parallel divergencies in the case of the two poems from the established conventions—in this instance those of the Court of Love—which underlie both," concludes convincingly that the "framework, the cadre of the *Paradys* is in striking agreement with that of the second part of the B-version

[1] Englische Studien, Vol. XXVI, p. 321, 1879.

of the *Prologue* of the *Legend of Good Women*." Moreover, since the common celebration of the daisy comes in
each poem to a focus in a ballade, and these ballades show
striking similarities in function and in treatment, and
since Chaucer knew and had already borrowed from the
Paradys d'Amour as long before as 1369, Lowes concludes
that Froissart's poetry, as well as that of Deschamps and
Machault, was familiar to Chaucer and consciously, or un-
consciously influenced him.[2]

In 1386 Froissart began again his wanderings in Au-
vergne and Flanders searching out stories for his chronicles. In Flanders, Froissart's sympathies were so thoroughly aroused by the accounts of the ruined merchants
and mechanics of Ghent that he devoted many pages of his
Second Book, which he completed in 1387, to the Flemish
troubles alone.

From this period on, Froissart spent his days visiting
from court to court, gaining new data and verifying the
old. The following passage reveals how conscientious he
was in his search for information:

" I had, thanks to God, sense, memory, good remembrance of
everything, and an intellect clear and keen to seize upon the acts
which I could learn. I have followed and frequented the company
of diverse nobles and great lords, as well in France, England and
Scotland as in diverse countries, and have knowledge by them and
always to my power justly have inquired for the truth of the
deeds of war and adventures that have fallen—every night, as
soon as we were at our lodgings, I wrote ever all that I heard in
the day, the better thereby to have the remembrance. . . ."

At Orthez in 1388, Gaston Phebus, Count of Fois, received
him graciously and invited him to read *Méliador* aloud

---

[2] *The Prologue to the Legend of Good Women as related to the
French Marguerite poems and the Filostrato.* Publications of the
Modern Language Association, Vol. XIX, p. 393.

during the evening, when "nobody dared to say a word
because he wished me to be heard, such delight did he take
in listening." So reading, relating things he had heard
and noting the reports of others, he went through Tou-
louse and Avignon to Valenciennes where he composed in
1390 his third book, *The Chronicle of Portugal*, and began
his fourth. But finding his notes incomplete on the affairs
of Castile and Portugal, he hastened away to Bruges, a
great commercial center of the Portuguese. There learning that a well informed Portuguese knight was just start-
ing for Prussia, Froissart at once followed, and for six days,
note-book in hand absorbed the desired information. Such
was his zeal. But from such eagerness we must not conclude that Froissart had much historic sense. His interest
was obviously romantic, rather than scientific, and he cared
only to paint a vivid picture of the events of the fourteenth
century with portraits of people as they appeared to him,
no more. He was a chronicler, not a critic, and his livelihood depended on his patrons. Moreover, inasmuch as he
was a Fleming, not an Englishman, or a Frenchman, leni-
ency may be urged for his unstable sympathies.

In 1391, Froissart left his patron, Gui de Blois, and
journeyed to Paris, and thence three years later, he embarked once more for England. His forty-year absence
had done much to estrange him from even his friends. He
found the country in upheaval, and King Richard II, besieged on all sides by commons and nobles, in imminent
danger of losing the crown. Nevertheless the old chronicler gained favor with the king by presenting a copy of
his *traités amoureux*, a "fayre boke well covered with
velvet, garnysshed with clasps of silver and gylte. Whanne
the Kynge opened it, it pleased hym well, for it was fayre
enlumyned and written and covered with crymson velvet

with ten botons of sylver and gylte, and roses of golde in the myddes, wyth two great clapses gylte rychely wrought. Than the Kyng demanded me wherof it treated, and I shewed hym how it treated of maters of love; wherof the kyng was glad and loked in it and reed yt in many places, for he could speke and rede French very well. . . ." During his sojourn in England, Froissart gathered the material for his fourth book from the Dukes of York and Gloucester and others at court. Although pleased with his reception, Froissart could not avoid seeing the discontent of the people and hearing their murmurs against Richard's misrule. Still loyal to him, however, he left England in dejection and, returning to France, began to complete the fourth and last book of the Chronicles. This part covers the years 1389–1400, and gives a vivid account of the beginning of the Civil Wars,—a narrative which, as will be seen, made a vivid impression upon Elizabethan writers. On learning with horror of the abdication and death of Richard II, Froissart abruptly concluded the fourth book with a description of the funeral of the wretched king.

During the next ten years illness, perhaps, forced him to abandon his pen, but when temporary strength returned he felt obliged to revise again the first book of the Chronicles. In a style quite different from the original version, he rewrote that part of his history which he had first written under the influence of Jean le Bel's Chronicles. This last redaction, extant in one manuscript in Rome, concludes at 1350, and is enlivened not only by disgressions and reminiscences, but by a savage attack upon the English people, and an elegy on the unhappy monarch who had honored him a few years before. Finally, as if in remembrance of old days and happier times, he paid glowing tribute to the memory of his former patroness, Queen Philippa.

The rest is but tradition which reads that Froissart died at Chimay in the year 1410, desperately poor and lonely. No friend, as far as we can learn, ever carved his name on a gravestone, or left a word of regret for the death of the greatest chronicler of the Middle Ages.

CHAPTER II

LORD BERNERS AND HIS TRANSLATION

1

The reputation of John Bourchier, second Lord Berners, according to Fuller's *Worthies of Hertfordshire,* was that of a "marshall man, well seen in all military discipline"; and the Letters and State Papers of King Henry VIII bear witness to his active life both as warrior and statesman.[1] By posterity, however, Berners is remembered chiefly as the translator of French history and romance. Born in Tharfield, Hertfordshire, in 1467, or 1469, he came from a long line of noble ancestors. His great grandfather joined the royal family by marrying Anne, daughter of Thomas of Woodstock, the sixth son of Edward III. John Bourchier, grandfather of Lord Berners, attended Parliament with the baronage in 1455, and fought in the battle of St. Albans for the house of Lancaster under Henry VI. Later, joining the house of York, he was appointed Constable of Windsor Castle by Edward IV. His eldest son, Humphrey Bourchier, married Elizabeth Tylney, who bore him three children, John Bourchier, the subject of the present sketch, and two daughters, Margaret and Anne. In 1471, the father was killed in the battle of Barnet while fighting for Edward IV. A few years later Lady Berners married Thomas Howard, Duke of Norfolk, and it sems probable that young John Bourchier received his early training under the guardianship of his step-father. On the death of his grandfather the lad succeeded to the title of Baron Berners

[1] Brewer's Letters and Papers I–VIII.

14

(Barners, or Barnes, as variously spelled). According to
Antony à Wood, he entered Balliol College, Oxford, and
afterwards traveled on the continent throughout the tur-
bulent reign of Richard III. During his sojourn abroad,
the Bourchier family became alienated from the house of
York, and gave their assistance to Henry of Richmond.
At the accession of Richmond as Henry VII, Cardinal
Bourchier, Archbishop of Canterbury, and great uncle of
Lord Berners, performed the coronation ceremonies.

In 1477 on the marriage of one of the royal princes,
Berners received his knighthood, and in 1492 engaging ''to
serve the king in his warres beyond see on hole yeere
with two speres'' he participated in the siege of Boulogne.
He was first summoned to Parliament by the title ''John
Bourgchier, lord of Berners'' in the eleventh year of Henry
VII, and on the accession of Henry VIII he immediately
became his trustworthy official, acting as a commissioner of
peace for Hertfordshire, and two years later for Surrey.
From time to time from 1511 on, Berners borrowed sums of
money from Henry VIII, and owed in the December of
that year a debt of 350 pounds, which later caused him
great embarrassment.

In 1513 he journeyed to Calais in the centre division as
captain of the King's guard and conducted himself with
bravery at the siege of Tourenne. His deed of special
merit seems to have been the recovery of a gun that had
been left behind on the road by negligence and had nearly
fallen into the hands of the French. In the fall of the
same year he marshalled the army in Scotland, where he
doubtless fought in the battle of Flodden Field. On May
18, 1514, he was granted the reversion of Chancellor of the
Exchequer on the death or surrender of Thomas Lovell;
and toward the close of the year he acted as Chamberlain
to the English Queen of France at the marriage of the
King's sister, Mary, to Louis XII.

At some unrecorded date Lord Berners married Catherine, daughter of John Howard, Duke of Norfolk, the sister-in-law of his mother. By her he had two daughters Mary and Jane. He also had several natural children.

In 1516 the office of Chancellor of the Exchequer reverted to him, and adorned in his robes of office he sat for Hans Holbein. The portrait reveals Lord Berners as large and thick-set with magnificent chest and shoulders. Mild frank eyes look out from a massive head, adorned with a broad hat. His face is smooth shaven, but his long straight hair falls to the short neck and encircles strong mastiff jaws. Below his large hawk-like nose, his full lips turn impressively and grimly down. Partly concealed in his right hand is a lemon—a fruit then greatly valued for warding off the plague.

With the Archbishop of Armagh in 1518, Berners journeyed as special ambassador to Spain to promulgate a treaty between Charles and Henry VIII. But he was so severely attacked with gout that the Archbishop was obliged to conduct the affairs alone, while Berners wrote letters to the King describing bull-fights and other entertainments at the Spanish court. Since the negotiations dragged on from April to December, he also sent repeated requests for money to enable him to live in accord with an ambassador's rank and dignity. In July he wrote to Wolsey: "God send hit an ende, for we lye here with most charge and expence, horse and man, and in most scarcitie of all things as well meate as drink that may be thought." Because of his illness he desired to return to England as far as possible by land, but the funds were so scanty that he was finally compelled to take the nearest way, and in January, 1519, he left the Spanish court and embarked at St. Sebastian. A year later with his wife he attended King Henry at the Field of the Cloth of Gold, and on July

2, 1520, he received the thanks of the Privy Council for a description of this ceremony.

But the most active days of Lord Berners' public life were drawing to a close; his health was still poor; his debts were unpaid; and he desired retirement from military service. In 1520 a vacancy occurring in the governorship of Calais, he gladly received the appointment from the King with 100 pounds yearly for his own use, and 104 pounds as "spyall money"—an income which afforded him leisure for the literary work which he desired to undertake.

According to his own confession, history, whether relating fact or fiction, had always been Lord Berners' literary passion. In this respect he virtually bears the same relationship to history and romance as his more distinguished predecessor, William Caxton, and he is perhaps the most important contributor after Caxton to the great vogue of histories and French romances which continued in England through the late fifteenth and early sixteenth centuries. How extensive was the passion for medieval lore in contrast with classical antiquity is well illustrated by the output from Caxton's press. Its total production reaches above 18,000 folio pages and among these volumes there is not the text of a single work of classical antiquity. Moreover, the few translations of Greek and Latin writers are nearly all at secondhand from French versions.

Caxton has often been blamed for not issuing the English Bible, or the Greek and Latin classics for the use and instruction of the people, but such criticism fails to comprehend the tastes of the reading public for which Caxton printed. On account of the series of political catastrophes and civil wars, the English knew very little of the refinements of the French culture which Chaucer had portrayed. "In most of their persevering studies" says W. P. Ker, "they are little better than the ambitious gallants in Elizabethan comedy, whose education has been neglected, the Gullios, who learn manners by the book of compliments. Nothing in history is more desperate than the attempts of English writers under the Plantagenets to master the secrets of French courtliness.'' Just when the medieval tradition was about to disappear forever Caxton preserved it by issuing that monument of courtly lore, the *Morte d'Arthur,* and other numerous romances, and conduct books, which he could hardly print fast enough to satisfy the requests of the gentle folk. Moreover, as Caxton himself tells us in *Charles the Great,* he was obliged to earn his livelihood from the publications of his press; they would have yielded little had he not supplied the popular demand. The wealthy and learned classes were made up almost wholly of clergy and nobility. He provided psalters, directories, and moral tales like the Golden Legend for the former and for the latter, romances of chivalry and books of courtly conduct. His ardent appeal to the knighthood of England in the *Order of Chivalry* is another noteworthy indication alike of his own personal enthusiasm and of the spirit of the age. Not to comment on his inestimable service to English literature by his editions of Chaucer, Lydgate and others, his contribution to English history may well be noted in connection with that of Lord Berners. He issued the only available histories in English prose, the *Brute,* or the *Chronicles of England;* and the *Polychronicon,* which he continued nearly to his own time.

In view of Caxton's intimate acquaintance with medieval French literature, it is surprising that the chronicles of Froissart had to await translation into English until over thirty years after Caxton's death. It is unbelievable that he was ignorant of a history that related with such brilliancy the illustrious deeds of the English in the Hundred Years War. That he was acquainted with it seems evident from a reference in his *Order of Chivalry* to the *Roman au Chroniques* (which he classes with the romances of *Lancelot* and *Percival*), a title by which Froissart's history was first commonly known.

This title, *Roman au Chroniques,* moreover, is another indication of the attitude of the age towards history. Romance in those days was not necessarily considered fiction, and it received admission without cavil into chronicle writing. *Morte d'Arthur,* for example, or *Huon of Bordeaux,* was as authentic history to its readers as Froissart, even though Froissart's was by far the greatest history of the time conceived and written in this romantic vein. Full as it is of anachronisms, apocryphal incidents and imaginary conversations, it nevertheless reveals the actual men and manners of the time, and recreates the spirit of the past more successfully than the careful details of any other historian.

This extensive vogue of romance and history thus nourished by Caxton and Malory was fostered by their successor, Lord Berners, shortly after he received the appointment of Governor of Calais. He was doubtless drawn to Froissart's work largely by its romantic appeal, for like Caxton, Berners fervently voices the same admiration and passion for chivalry, and hopes his translation may be the means of inspiring and guiding youth to the performing of "famous actes and glorious dedes." Moreover, he was encouraged in this enormous undertaking by Henry VIII, who commanded him to make the translation. The first volume occupied three years, and he sent the manuscript over to England to be issued by Pynson in January, 1523. The second volume, completed two years and a half later, was issued from Pynson's press in August, 1525. Thus what Malory and Caxton had done for England by rescuing some of the famous romances of the thirteenth century, Berners did for history by translating Froissart.

But his enthusiasm for romantic literature was not quenched, for he immediately set to work translating *Huon of Bordeaux*. This he undertook at the request of the Earl of Huntington, just as Caxton several years before had received orders for similar works from "dyverse gentlemen" and even a king and a princess. The romance, issued by Caxton's successor, Wynkyn de Worde, in 1534, was widely read by Elizabethan writers and furnished story for Spenser, Greene and Shakespeare.

The hystory of the moost noble and valyaunt knyght Arthur of lytell brytagne, Berners' next translation, was printed without date after his death by Robert Redborne. Even the translator himself shows a slight scepticism in his preface regarding this romance, for he writes that the heroes "overcame many harde and straunge adventures the whiche as to our humayne reason sholde seme to be incredible. Wherefore after that I had begon this sayd processe, I had determined to have left and gyven up my laboure, for I thoughte it sholde have ben reputed but a folye in me to translate be seming suche a fayned mater, wherin semeth to be so many unpossybylytees." Calling to mind, however, that other romances portrayed heroes performing supernatural deeds, Berners took courage with the faith that the author "devysed it not without some maner of trouthe or vertuous entent."

The last translations of Lord Berners contributed to another literary fashion that Caxton had catered to—the courtly conduct book. As from romantic history Berners had passed to pure romance, so from romance he was attracted by the new Spanish conduct books of Guevara and Diego de San Pedro, still in favor among the nobility. At the request of Lady Elizabeth Carew, he translated the *Castle of Love*, and Sir Francis Bryan, his nephew, issued the *Golden Book of Marcus Aurelius*.[2]

Although these extensive literary pursuits are proof that Berners spent large amounts of time at his desk in the deputy general's office, there are abundant evidences that he did not neglect his official duties. The state papers of Henry VIII contain numerous letters from him to Cardinal Wolsey and other officials of the court pertaining always to the fortifications, the manoeuvres of the French armies, or the arrival of visitors of note that he entertained. Among his visitors in 1522 was Charles V then on his way to England.

The last years of Berners' life were filled with increasing anxieties over his health and finances. From the time of his visit to Spain in 1518, he seems to have been susceptible to severe attacks of gout which sometimes incapacitated him for several months. Moreover, his debts to Henry, still unpaid, had increased to 500 pounds. To add further to his troubles, he became involved in a series of law suits over his estates and property in Hertfordshire; and Henry, at all times no lenient creditor, began pressing him for his dues. Berners vainly endeavored to mollify the King by frequent gifts of hawks, but even while Berners was lying upon his death bed, Henry, with seemingly greedy haste, sent over special agents to attach his personal property. Nor when the death of Berners followed on March 16, 1533, did Henry pay any respect to his memory. He immediately placed Berners' property under arrest and ap-

[2] Since there are several good studies of Berners' version of Guevara in relation to the development of English Euphuism, it does not seem necessary to repeat here a discussion that is generally familiar. Cf. Bond, Lyly, Vol. I; Child, John Lyly and Euphuism; Lee on Lyly in D.N.B.

pointed a successor to his office. The elaborate inventory
of Berners' possessions in the record office witnesses the
grandeur in which he lived at Calais. One entry of espe-
cial interest in the inventory of his property reads: ''Item
in the stody $\frac{xx}{iiij}$ books vz oon of Latten and frenche,''—
but unfortunately no details regarding this library are
recorded.

The life of Lord Berners thus reveals years of distinguished activity in several spheres. He was a trusted
ambassador and governor, skilled in diplomacy and poli-
tics; he was a worthy knight in various exploits of war,
whether as a member of the King's bodyguard, or marshall
of the army; and always that for which he holds a secure,
if minor place among the literary worthies of the sixteenth
century, namely, an ardent lover and translator of romance
and history, who ''rescued as much as he could of the
treasures of the Middle Ages before they were overwhelmed
by the new learning.''

2

THE TRANSLATION OF FROISSART

It was at the command of the same ungrateful King
who hovered over his deputy's death bed to snatch his
property, that Berners had undertaken several years before the translation of the chronicles of Froissart. In casting about for French editions of the chronicles to translate, Berners was confronted with a wide choice, for no less
than five editions had been issued between the death of
Froissart in 1410 and the arrival of Lord Berners at Calais
in 1520. Moreover, it was assuredly fitting, if not impera-
tive that Berners should choose those redactions and versions of the chronicles that Froissart had written in the
early years before he became thoroughly hostile to every-

thing English. The first printed edition of Froissart in the original was published at Paris for Antoine Verard in 1495, and the second for Verard in 1497. Others appearing at intervals of several years bear the dates 1505, 1513, 1518. A close examination and comparison of the five French editions with Berners' text show that the translator employed the second edition of Verard, 1497, containing Froissart's original version of the first book of chronicles, which portrayed the battles of Crecy and Poitiers with a spirit and sympathy thoroughly English and gave the English people the first worthy narratives of their illustrious past.

The appearance of Lord Berners' translation of Froissart in 1523–5 marks also a new epoch in the writing of English history. None of the crude attempts at chronicling in the thirteenth or fourteenth centuries can bear comparison with the distinguished history of Chaucer's contemporary. The numerous Latin chronicles were written for the most part by monks living remotely from the bustle of the world who never had come in contact with the blaze of chivalry, or gossiped for information with knights and heralds. Had there been an English Froissart in the 13th and 14th centuries, the chances are many that he would have written in Latin, for English prose had not yet come to its own, in spite of the brave, though crude efforts, such as the *Brute*, and Trevisa's translation of Higden's *Polychronicon*. Not until many years had passed could Berners prove that it was possible to write like Froissart in English. And a genuine English Froissart Berners provided, with the spirit and style of the original admirably and faithfully preserved. When writing, however, on his own account, Berners fashioned after the manner of the new school, an ornate style of his own, full of antitheses and wearisome repetitions; but when he translated Froissart, he usually followed his original "so well that if his text were retranslated faithfully, the very style of Froissart would reappear."[3]   By such a statement Jusserand doubtless does not imply that in all respects Berners produced an accurate, or literal translation, for just as the French publishers of the printed French editions had felt free in many instances to abbreviate or to adapt at will the numerous manuscripts at their disposal, so Berners did not hesitate to make free with the text of his Verard edition. He was fully aware of his deficiencies in French and he offered a timely apology for his mistranslations (which extend occasionally to such simple words as the days of the week), "requyrynge all the reders and herers thereof to take this my *rude translacion in gre.*"   Again he often made mistakes in the names of places and persons, usually rendering them literally, even though he must have known that some of them were wrong.   Sometimes, on the other hand, he ventured corrections of his own and occasionally erred in his changes.   Recent editors have consequently had serious difficulties with identification.   One editor fittingly speaks of Berners' "Hell of Proper names"—an epithet exceedingly appropriate to those who have labored over the egregious misspellings first of Froissart, then of the scribes and printers, then of Berners, and finally of Pynson, or Middleton.   Only on occasion does the English text spell a proper name twice alike, and this practice when extended to common words gives the printed page a startling, as well as quaint appearance.

The prose of Lord Berners' translation of Froissart, like that of Caxton and other contemporaries, exhibits as has been noted two distinct styles—the simple and picturesque, when he faithfully follows the lucid style of Froissart; and the highly elaborate, artificial style, when he attempts any-

[3] Jusserand, Lit. Hist. of Eng. People, Vol. I, pp. 404 ff.

thing original like a preface or a dedication that must be imposing and elegant. Since he realizes that he is insufficient in "the facondyous arte of rethoryke," he does not presume that he has "reduced it into fresshe ornate polysshed Englysshe." At this time when English prose was making its troubled way among the purists of the Ascham Wilson school on the one hand, and the innovators of the Guevara school on the other, Berners deserves credit for steering a sane middle course, and for keeping more closely to the medieval tradition though not allowing his expression to be hampered by the precise and formal periods of the classical models. In respect to syntax and sentence structure, Berners' prose resembles that of the fourteenth rather than the sixteenth century. It is neither pure nor accurate, and his expressions are often careless and involved. "Berners' sentences are sometimes begun, broken off, begun again, and after all never ended; verbs are left without subjects and relatives without antecendents; grammatically the style is often hopeless. . . ."[4] Such a passage will serve well to illustrate these deficiencies:

" Ye haue harde riht well here before, howe the Kyng of Nauer, who hadde to his wyfe the frenche kynges suster, for the loue of the one and of the other, it was sayd and purposed, that the herytage of the chyldren of the Kyng of Nauer, the whiche was fallen to them by the ryght of their mother, yt the french kyng their vncle, by the succession of his suster, ought to haue power thereof in the name of the chyldren, seyng the chyldren were in his kepynge, wherby all the lande that the Kynge of Naver held in Normandy shulde be in ye french Kynges hand, as long as his nephewes were within age."

But it is manifestly unfair to take Lord Berners' style at its worst, for only occasionally does his power of clear expression lapse into confusion, and under the guidance of

4 G. C. Macaulay, Chronicles of Froissart, Introd., p. xxi.

Froissart's original, he can write terse, virile and graphic prose. Excelled perhaps by Malory and Caxton for directness and lucidity, he is yet more virile than either, and it requires only a few comparisons of his text with that of Johnes, his nineteenth century successor, to observe the difference between prose with, and prose without style. For example Berners translates:

" The horses whan they felt ye sharpe arowes, they would in no wyse go forward, but drewe backe, and flang and toke on so feersly, that many of them fell on their maisters."

Johnes renders the passage:

" The horses smarting under pain of the wounds made by their bearded arrows, would not advance, but turned about, and by their unruliness threw their masters."

The superiority of Berners is again clear in the following:

" The constable defended hymselefe valyauntly with that wepyn that he had; howbeit, his defense hadde vayled hym but lytell, and the great grace of god had nat ben; styll he sate on his horse tyll he hed a full stroke on ye heed, with whiche stroke he fell fro his horse ryght agaynst a baker's dore, who was up and busy to bake breed, and had left his dore halfe open. . . ."

Johnes translates:

" The constable parried the blows tolerably well with his short cutlass; but his defense would have been of no avail, if God's providence had not protected him. He kept steady on horseback sometime, until he was villianously struck on the back part of his head, which knocked him off his horse. In his fall he hit upon the hatch of a baker's door, who was already up to attend his business and to bake his bread."

We more especially commend Lord Berners' good taste when we pass from the simple style of the translation, and read the ornate style in which he wrote the dedication and preface of the chronicles. Feeling doubtless the demand of the time for cultivated rhetoric and fine writing, he desired to enrich his expression as much as possible. For this reason, he is classed with Caxton among the innovators, since he practices word borrowing extensively and its complementary device, amplification. With his successors Lyly, Nashe and the others, he is guilty of Wilson's charge of trying to catch "an ynkehorne terme by the taile." Whenever he adapts, or borrows words from the French, he couples them with as many equivalents as he can think of—a device which soon becomes a great burden. He does not, however, carry it to the ridiculous extent of William Sommer in the letter that Wilson deprecates.[5] Sommer writes:

"Ponderyng, expending and reuoluting with myself, your ingent affabilitie and ingenious capacity for mundaine affaires: I cannot but celebrate & extol your magnifical dexteritie aboue all other."

Berners writes:

"Thus whan I aduertysed and remembred the many-folde comodyties of hystorie, howe benefyciall it is to mortall folke and eke howe laudable and merytoryous a dede it is to write hystories, fixed my mynde to do some thyng therein: and euer wha this ymaginacyon came to me, I volued, tourned, and redde many volumes and bokes, conteynyng famouse histories. . . ."[6]

On the other hand, there is cause for satisfaction that Berners did not yield to the pressure for fine writing so far as to render the translation of Froissart in the ornate style. The entire prologue, however, is well worth quoting in full, not only because of its philological interest, as an

[5] The Arte of Rhetorique, G. H. Mair, Oxford, 1909, p. 163.
[6] Preface to Vol. I.

example of Berners' style in courtly dress; but also for the
picture it discloses of Berners' mind,—his enthusiasm, and
his reverent spirit for the great heroes that have gone, and
the wondrous deeds they have performed; his lofty devotion to chivalric ideals; and his eagerness that the noble
youth should be fostered with the incalculable virtues of
history:

" What condygne graces and thankes ought men to gyue to the
writers of historyes, who with their great labours haue done so
moche profyte to the humayne lyfe; they shewe, open, manifest
and declare to the reder, by example of olde antyquite, what we
shulde enquere, desyre, and folwe; and also, what we shulde
eschewe, auoyde, and utterly flye: for whan we (beynge vnexpert
of chauces) se, beholde, and rede the auncyent actes, gestes, and
dedes, howe and with what labours, daugers, and paryls they were
gested and done, they right greatly admonest, ensigne and teche
us howe we may lede forthe our lyues: and farther, he that hath
the perfyte knowledge of others ioye, welthe, and highe prosperite,
and also trouble, sorowe, and great aduersyte, hath thexpert
doctryne of all parylles.   And albeit, that mortall folke are mar-
veylously separated both by lande and water, and right wonder-
ously sytuate, yet are they and their actes (done peradventure by
the space of a thousande yere) copact togyder by thistographier,
as it were, the dedes of one selfe cyte, and in one manes lyfe:
wherefore I say, that historie may well be called a diuyne prouy-
dence; for as the celestyall bodyes above complecte all and at
every tyme the vniuersall worlde, the creatures therin coteyned,
and all their dedes, sembably so do—the history.   Is it nat a
right noble thynge for vs by the fautes and errours of other, to
amēde and erect our lyfe into better?   We shulde nat seke and
acquyre that other dyd; but what thyng was most best, most
laudable, and worthely done, we shulde putte before our eyes to
folowe.   Be nat the sage counsayles of two or thre olde fathers
in a cyte, towne, or coūtre, whome long age hath made wyse,
dyscrete and prudent, far more praysed, lauded and derely loued
than of the yonge menne?   Howe mache more than ought hys-

tories to be cōmended, praysed, and loued, in whom is encluded so many sage counsayls, great reasons and hygh wisedoms of so innumerable persons, of sundry nacyons, and of euery age, and that in so long space as four or fyue hundred yere. The most profytable thyng in this worlde for the instytution of the humayne lyfe is hystorie. Ones the contyuuall redyng therof maketh yonge men equall in prudence to olde men; and to olde fathers stryken in age it mynystreth experyence of thynges. More, it yeldeth priuate persons worthy of dignyte, rule, and gouernaunce; it compelleth themperours, hygh rulers, and gouernours to do noble dedes, to thende they may optayne immortall glory; it exciteth, moueth, and stereth the strong hardy warriours, for the great laude that they haue after they ben deed, promptly to go in hande with great and harde parels, in defence of their countre; and it prohibyteth reprouable persons to do mischeuous dedes, for feare of infamy and shame; so thus, through the monumentes of writynge whiche is the testymony vnto vertue, many men haue ben moued, some to bylde cytes some to deuyse and establishe lawes right profitable, necessarie, and behouefull for the humayne lyfe: some other to fynde newe artes, craftes, and sciences, very requisyte to the vse of mākynde, but aboue all thynges, wherby mans welthe ryseth, speciall laude and cause ought to be gyuen to historie: it is the keper of suche thinges as haue been vertuously done and the wytnesse of yuell dedes: and by the benefite of hystorie all noble, highe, and vertuous actes be immortall. What moued the strong and ferse Hercules to entrpryse in his lyfe so many great incōparable labours and paryls? Certaynly nought els but $_y{}^t$ for his meryt immortalyte mought be gyuen to hym of all folke. In sēblable wyse dyd his imytator, noble duke Thesus, and many other innumerable worthy prices and famouse men, whose vertues ben redemed frō oblyuion and shyne by historie. And whereas other monuments in processe of tyme, by varyable chaunces, are confused and lost: the vertue of hystory dyfussed and spredde throughe the vnyuersall worlde, hath to her custos and kepar, it (that is to say, tyme), whiche cosumeth the other writynges. And albeit that those menne are right worthy of great laude and prayse, who by their writynges shewe and lede vs the waye to vertue: yet neuerthelesse, the poems, lawes, and other actes that they foūde deuysed and writ, ben mixed with some domage: and sō-tyme for the trueth they ensigne a man to lye: but onelye historie, truely with wordes, representying the actes, gestes, and dedes done complecteth all profyte; it moveth, stereth, and compelleth to honestie; detesteth, erketh, and abhorreth vices: it extolleth, enhaunceth, and lyfteth vp suche as ben noble and vertuous; depresseth, poystereth, and thrusteth downe such as ben wicked, yuell, and reprouable.   What knowledge shulde we haue of auncyent thynges past, and historie were nat? whiche is the testymony thereof, the lyght of trouthe, the maystres of the lyfe humayne, the presydent remembraūce, and the mesanger of antiquyte.   Why moued and stered Phaleryus, the Kynge Phtholome, oft and dilygently to rede bokes?   Forsothe for none other cause, but that those thynges are founde writen in bokes, that the frēdes dare nat shewe to the prīce.   Moche more I wolde fayne write of the incomparably profyte of hystorie, but I feare me that I shulde to sore tourment the reder of this my preface; and also I doute nat but that the great vtilyte therof is better knowen than I coulde declare; wherfore I shall breuely come to a poynt.   Thus, whan I aduertysed and remembred the many-folde comodyties of hystorie, howe benefyciall it is to mortall folke and eke howe laudable and merytoryous a dede it is to write hystories, fixed my mynde to do some thyng terin; and euer wha this ymaginacyon came to me, I volued, tourned, and redde many volumes and bokes, conteyning famouse histories, and amonge all other.   I redde dilygently the four volumes or bokes of Sir Johan Froyssart of the country of Heynaulte, written in the Frenche tonge, whiche I iudged comodyous, necessarie, and profytable to be hadde in Englysshe, siths they treat of the fomous actes done in our parties; that is to say, in England, Frauce, Spaygne, Portyngale, Scotlade, Bretayne, Flauders, and other places adioyning; and especially they redounde to the honoure of Englysshe-men.   What pleasure shall it be to the noble gētylmen of England to se, beholde, and rede the highe enterprises, famous actes, and glorious dedes done and atchyued by their valyant auceytours?   Forsothe and God, this hath moued me at the highe comaundement of my moost redouted souerayne lorde Kynge Henry the VIII Kung of Englande and of Fraunce, and highe defender of the christen faythe, &c, under his gracyous supportacyon to do my deuoyre to translate out of the frenche into our maternall englysshe tonge the sayd volumes of sir Johan Froyssart; whiche cronycle begynneth at the raygne of the moost noble and valynt kynge edwarde the thyrde, the yere of our lorde a thousande thre hundred and sixtene and countynueth to the begynning of the reyne of King Henry the fourth, the yere of our lorde god a thousande and foure hundred: the space bytwene is threscore and fourtene yeres; requyrynge all the reders and herers therof to take this my rude translacion in gre.   And in that I haue nat folowed myne authour worde by worde, yet I trust I have ensewed the true reporte of the sentence of the mater; and as for the true namyng of all maner of personages, countries, cyties, townes, or feldes, whereas I coulde nat name them properly nor aptely in Englysshe, I have written them accordynge as I founde them in frenche; and thoughe I have nat gyuen every lorde, knyght, or squyer his true addycion, yet I trust I haue nat swarued fro the true sentēce of the mater.   And there as I haue named the dystaunce bytwene places by myles and leages, they must be vnderstande accordyng to the custome of the coūtris where as they be named, for in some place they be lengar than in some other; in Englande a leage or myle is well knowen; in Fraūce a leage is two myles, and in some place thre; and in other coūtre is more or lesse; euery nacion hath sondrie customes.   And if any faute be in this my rude translacyon, I remyt the correctyon thereof to thē that discretely shall fynde any reasonable defaute; and in their so doynge. I shall pray god to sende thē blysse of heuen.   Amen."

3

VOGUE OF THE TRANSLATION

In spite of all its crudities, however, the translation of Froissart remains a brave and noble prose monument.   Its vivid pictures of a brilliant epoch in feudal history aided in recreating the age of chivalry, and nourished the romantic and knightly sentiments of the time. Moreover its relation to immediate history is significant. Henry VIII was especially eager during the early twenties that his followers should be reconciled to the heavy taxes that the contemplated war with France would entail. In spite of his large and ostentatious professions of friendship with Francis I, at the Field of the Cloth of Gold in 1520, Henry was entering into a secret coalition with Pope Leo X and Charles V of Spain against the French monarch. In November 1521, the articles of agreement were completed and Henry began an aggressive war against France in the summer of the following year. As the untold luxuries of his court had already drained the vast treasures which his penurious and foreseeing father had accumulated, Henry was obliged to levy severe and unjust taxes to finance the hostilities he had begun. No literary work could have been better suited to arouse the ambitions of the English warriors than Berners' brilliant pages recounting the glories of England under Edward III, and the daring engagements of the Black Prince at Poitiers. Would not true Englishmen be filled with shame at the memory of those provinces that had formerly belonged to Normandy, and eagerly contribute to a new conquest for regaining their lawful lands? That Henry's purpose succeeded is shown by the preface to Berners' second volume: "and herin his hyghnesse taketh syngular pleasure to beholde howe his worthy subjettes seyng in hystorie the very famous dedes, a it were ymages, represent their valyaunt auncettours, contende by vigorous vertue and manhode to folowe, yea to passe them if they maye."

Even greater was the stimulus that the chronicle gave to the reading and writing of history. It has justly been said that Lord Berners' translation of Froissart was the first really important work printed in the English language relating to modern history. Eclipsing in literary merit all other previous chronicles it brought home a wealth of information respecting the relation of England to the continent in the fourteenth century, the wars of Edward III in Scotland and France, and the troublous vicissitudes of the reign of Richard II.

At least two editions were issued from Pynson's press, both bearing the same date. Between 1542 and 1547 William Middleton also issued an edition "in Fletestrete at the syne of the George," and containing the words affixed to the King's title "of the Church of England and also of Irelande in earth supreme heede,"—a title that Henry assumed in 1542. Since Middleton's activity as a printer fell between the years 1541 and 1547, the conjectural date 1533 of G. C. Macaulay is too early. To increase the confusion of editions some copies of Middleton's edition are extant, containing leaves from Pynson's press, a fact which would indicate that perhaps Middleton bought Pynson's old stock and issued another edition.

The following passage from the preface to the second volume shows that the translation was popular in England, for Berners says "The great pleasure that my noble countreymenne of Englande take in redyng the worthy and knightly dedes of their valyaunt auncettours encorageth me. . . ."

Moreover the translation of Froissart seems, according to one authority, to have made Berners' name famous, for in Bale's edition of Leland's *New Years Gift to King Henry VIII* describing that antiquarian's *Laboryouse Journey*,[7] printed in 1549, occurs this noteworthy sentence: "What els hath reduced the name of sir Johan Bourchier the lord Barners to a fame immortal, but hys translacyon of frossardes Chronycle from Frenche into Englyshe."

[7] Edited by Copinger, Manchester, 1895, p. 102.

4

His other writings also are elaborately cataloged under *Johannes Bourchier* in Bale's *Index Britanniae Scriptorum.*

Although the principal references to Berners' Froissart would naturally be found among books treating of historical matters, it would seem likely in view of its close relations with romance and with the development of English prose, to have merited the comment of the flourishing schools of style and language reformers on the one hand, and critics of historical writings on the other. Just why the translation received slight attention from both, is difficult to determine. Neither Ascham, who has strictures to make upon romance in his condemnation of Malory, as well as upon foreign influences in general, nor rhetoricians, like Wilson, who inveigh against inkhorn terms and oversea language, have aught to utter concerning the writing of Lord Berners. Even more surprising is the omission of his name among the numerous lists of English poets and historians, which writers of criticism included in, or appended to their discussions, e.g., the Scriptorum Catologus in Jonson's *Timber.* Peacham, who devotes a separate chapter to history in his *Compleat Gentleman,* does not refer to the translation. Bolton, who intended his *Hypercritica* to be complete, and who had very definite ideas as to how history should be written, casting blame upon Polydore Vergil, praising More, Speed, and Bacon, and alluding to Stowe and Holinshed, passes by Berners' Froissart in silence. Bolton apologizes, however, with the "hope now that no man will be so captious or ungentle as to make it a matter of quarrel to me, if I have left out any other for Want of Memory or Knowledge. . . ." It seems strange that a history cited so often, and so well known by the chroniclers and dramatists should have lapsed from knowledge or memory. Moreover, the same is true of Sidney's *Apology for Poetry* and Bacon's *Advancement of Learning,* both of which discourse with more or less fullness on the art of writing history. Sometimes even in contemporary catalogs of books where the English chronicles stand out in full array, Froissart's history is not mentioned.

Perhaps the reason for this neglect lies in the fact that the chronicles were invariably referred to as Froissart's and not as Lord Berners'. This is true of all the instances where the history is quoted by the English chronicles. On the margins, or in the lists of authorities at beginning or end, the name *Froissart* always appears, although in nearly every instance, as will be proved in the next chapter, the translation and not the original was employed. Continual reference to Froissart's chronicles in this way would be likely to obscure the name of the translator, who after all was merely a medium, and would lead, in spite of its English rendering, to the rightful consideration of the chronicle as the work of a foreigner, and a Frenchman. Hence it might easily be excluded from mention among English histories, more especially since it was virtually a detailed history of foreign as well as of English affairs. Perhaps it was for these reasons that the later critics of historical writing say nothing of Berners' Froissart. Many of them, moreover, wrote when the market was glutted with histories by English writers, and when the purely romantic conception of history was waning; and their search was for a more rational and philosophical treatment than had yet been written. Tested by such standards the chronicles of Froissart naturally left much to be desired.

But while rhetoricians and critics passed by Berners' Froissart in silence, other prose writers, not only the group of historians, and the antiquarian Leland, but also fiction writers like Painter and Nashe, made reference to Berners' translation. Painter referred to it in his *Palace of Pleas-*

ure,[8] and Nashe evidently possessed a copy in his library. In *Have With You to Saffron Waldon*[9] there are probable references to Berners' translation, and in the general discourse on spirits in *Terrors of the Night* (1594) Nashe writes: *"Froisard* saith, the Earl of *Fois* had a familiar that presented it selfe vnto him in the likenes of two rushes fighting one with another."

Four years later in the *Prayse of Red Herring*, Nashe refers to "father Froysard's" picturesque account of the banishment of Bolingbroke:

"O he is attended vpon most Babilonically, and Xerxes so ouercloyd not the Hellespont with his foystes, gallies, and brigandines, as he mantleth the narrow seas with his retinue, being not much behinde in the check-roule of his Ianissaries and contributories, with Eagle-soaring Bullingbroke, that at his remouing of houshold into banishment (*as father Froysard threapes vs doune*) was accompanied with 40,000 men, women, and children weeping, from London to the lands-end at Douer."[9]

By far the greatest contribution of Lord Berners' translation is found in the narratives of the reigns of Edward III and Richard II which the long series of English chroniclers from Hall to Speed adopt in varying degree. The following chapter shows how limited was knowledge of Froissart's history in England before the translation and how Berners practically introduced Froissart to compilers of English history and writers of Chronicle drama.

[8] Cf. subsequent chapter on Edward III, p. 63–4.

[9] Works, Mackerrow, London, I, p. 350; III, p. 185, 187–8; V, p. 126 ff.

CHRONOLOGICAL OUTLINE FOR CHAPTER III

1516 Fabian's *Chronicle*.

1523–25 Berners' translation of Froissart.

1534 Polydore Vergil's *Historia Anglica*.

1542 Middleton's edition of Lord Berners' translation.

1548 Hall's *Chronicle*.

1567–68 Painter's *Palace of Pleasure*.

1568 Grafton's *Chronicle*, 2 vols.

1578 Holinshed's *Chronicles*.

1580 Stow's *Annales*.

CHAPTER III

FROISSART AND THE ENGLISH CHRONICLES

During the first eighty years of the sixteenth century the presses poured forth upon the Elizabethan public a flood of rival chronicles exalting England's illustrious past, all of them differing from one another, but all purporting to be authentic histories. The rivalry between chroniclers was often intense and bitter, and the clamor so great that rival compilers brought out new editions of their Summaries, Manuals, Surveys, or Chronicles at intervals on an average of every three years. Each new issue gave its writer his opportunity to sneer at the work of his rival and to reply in full to the acrimonious charges of plagiarism, or falsification that they had published against him in the prefaces of their editions. After 1580, although the chronicles still continued in demand, they had given birth to the brilliant series of chronicle plays that crowned the stage during the last two decades of Queen Elizabeth's reign.

The development of chronicle writing in England, as has been noted, was as slow as the development of English prose; and the standards throughout the period remained about the same. Almost every English chronicle is a compilation from innumerable chronicle sources and narrates sometimes baldly, sometimes literally what had been previously recorded. As the narrative descends to contemporary events the writer usually takes a new interest and handles his narrative in a more personal and graphic way. But rarely does he attempt anything more than a description of events in bald chronicle form; and too frequently he shows no power of selection or perspective, and no historical sense. He fills the work with long descriptions of royal or city feasts, entertainments, processions; with fabulous tales, scraps of poetry; or with matters more important to his mind than even foreign events, such as the remarkably cold winter of 1390, or the delivery of a monstrous child by a woman of Kent.

The reason for such crude narrative in the English chronicles lies partly in the character of the men who compiled them. Not infrequently they were tradesmen of little or no education, who as their wealth increased attained perhaps the rank of sheriff, or alderman. Fabian was a member of the Drapers Company; Grafton was a grocer who later became a distinguished printer. Jonson states that John Stow "had monstrous observations in his *Chronicle* and was of his craft a tailour." From such men as these it would be foolish to expect erudition or philosophical treatment of history. They reflected only the temper of the age with their moralizings on the Falls of Princes, and their beliefs that fiction of moral intent was as suitable as historical fact. Like their betters, the nobility and clergy, they exhibited the same scorn and contempt for the fickleness of the populace. Moreover, their extraordinary ambitions to write histories from the beginning of the world to their own times tended to preclude a thoughtful study or understanding of motives, of character, or of cause and effect. In this class we may put all the chronicles from Fabian's to Holinshed's and Stow's. Not until Bacon wrote his history of Henry VII in the next century did historical writing begin to receive philosophical treatment.

The critical sense, however, grows as the years pass by and expressions of dissatisfaction begin to appear in critical writings. In the *Apology for Poetry* (1595) Sidney voices his scorn of such a chronicler; "loden with old Mouse-eaten records, authorising himselfe (for the most part) vpon other histories, whose greatest authorities are built upon the notable foundation of Heare-say, hauing much-adoe to accord differing Writers and to pick trueth out of partiality, better acquainted with a thousande yeeres a goe then with the present age, and yet better knowing how his owne world goeth then how his owne wit runneth, curious for antiquities and inquisitive of nouelties, a wonder to young folkes and a tyrant in table talke, denieth, in a great chafe, that any man for teaching of vertue and vertuous actions is comparable to him. I am Lux vitae, Temporum magistra, Vita memoria, nuncia vetustatis, &c."

So later Bolton, in *Hypercritica* (1618), refers to "the vast vulgar Tomes procured for the most part by the hus-bandry of Printers and not by the appointment of the Prince or Authority of the Common-weal, in their tumul-tary and centonical Writings do seem to resemble some huge disproportionable Temple, whose Architect was not his Arts Master, but in which store of rich Marble, and many most goodly Statues, Columns, Arks, and antique Peices, recover'd from out of innumerable Ruins, are here and there in greater number then commendable order erected, with no Dispraise to their Excellencz, however, they were not happy in the Restorer."

Bad as these chronicles were from later points of view, they nevertheless brought home to the Elizabethans in an impressive way the downfalls and deaths of their royalty, and the viscissitudes of worldly things. In this connection the reigns of Edward III and Richard II held special interest for them, and the impression of both reigns con-veyed to them is largely that pictured by Froissart whose accounts of English affairs during these years (1325–1400) are particularly full and elaborate.

I

FRENCH VERSIONS OF FROISSART IN ENGLAND

Before the Elizabethan age, however, and before Berners had rendered Froissart into English, the influence of those French versions that found their way across the Channel had made itself felt, though traces of it are few in number and very hard to find. Perhaps the earliest instance is the contemporary poem, *Le Prince Noir,* written about 1835, by the herald of Sir John Chandos, a knight frequently described by Froissart as a friend of the Black Prince. That the herald was no ordinary man is shown by the retention of his title after his master's death and the important embassies afterwards entrusted to his care. It was part of the duty of heralds to keep a diary of events. In fact, as is well known, many of the romances of the fourteenth century were written by heralds, and Froissart states in his preface that he collected much of his material from them. Curiously enough there are evidences of resemblance between Chandos' Herald's poem and Froissart's chronicle which tend to show that the poet and the chronicler were either personally acquainted, or were familiar with each other's work. The very words of the Herald's interview with the Black Prince appear in Froissart.

Le Prince Noir is a poem in octasyllabics of over 4000 lines describing the life and famous exploits of the hero, portions of which the writer doubtless witnessed himself. Since the Herald and Froissart cover the same events in the course of their works, it is natural that the resemblances should be numerous. It seems probable that they met abroad, but the question nevertheless remains as to whether the poet was indebted to Froissart's *Chronicle* for any of his material. As early as 1361 Froissart presented a book to Queen Philippa during his visit to England. Conjecture presumes this gift to have been his early poetical version of the chronicles, unfortunately non-extant. Inasmuch as Froissart tells us in 1395 that he had not been in England for twenty-seven years, and as the Herald's poem was written perhaps before 1385, circumstances seem to preclude that the poem is indebted to the *Chronicles;* although it is possible that some of the manuscripts, either of the first volume of prose *Chronicles* of 1373, or of the two redactions of 1378 and 1383, had seen circulation in England and had come to the Herald's notice. However the matter is considered, there can be no question that the Herald was an original writer and no mere copyist; moreover the numerous differences in matters of detail between his poem and Froissart's chronicle seem to establish their independence of each other.[1]

Traces of the French chronicle in England during the turbulent fifteenth century are naturally wanting—the English people showing more concern for making history than for reading or writing it. Professor Child has cited[2] Froissart's brilliant account of Percy and Douglas as a source for the famous historical ballad, *The Battle of Otterburn,* which probably falls within this century. But evidences are wanting to establish any very close relation between the chronicle and the ballad literature of the period.

The chronicle histories of the fourteenth and fifteenth centuries as far as can be determined make no allusion to Froissart, nor employ his chronicle for the reigns of Edward III and Richard II. Thomas Walsingham had no need of sources, for he personally witnessed the latter part of the reign of Edward III and the whole of the career of Richard II; while other noteworthy contemporaries, Adam of Usk and Henry Knighton, also witnessed the events they

[1] For parallels and recent discussion see Oxford edition, 1910. Introd. lvi ff.

[2] F. J. Child's Collection of English Ballads, III, p. 289 ff.

described. *The Brute*, or *The Chronicles of England*, as it is sometimes called, is an independent English work compiled largely from London chronicles, deriving nothing from Froissart. The same is true of Trevisa and Capgrave. Nor in the private letters of the century such as the famous *Paston Letters*, in which books are often listed and described, is there any reference to the French chronicle. Only in Caxton's reference to the *Roman au Chroniques* in the last decade of the century is Froissart's work mentioned, and not until the second decade of the following century is it consulted as a source for fourteenth century history. Then the name of the old chronicler, *John Froyzarde*, appears in the list of authorities which Robert Fabian consulted for his *New Chronicles of England and France*.

Robert Fabian

Robert Fabian, a cloth merchant and member of the Drapers Company, and afterwards alderman of London, was the first English historian to offer something more elaborate and literary than the dull records of preceding writers, though he made little pretense of originality. His *New Chronicles of England and France* were published three years after his death in 1516. Because Fabian had no sense of historical proportion, he filled his narrative with trifling details, such as descriptions of feasts and bits of patriotic verse.

As sources for the conflicts between France and England from 1325 to 1400, Fabian employed two French histories, *Les Chroniques de France* (called the chronicle of St. Denis) issued at Paris in 1476; and the *Chronicles* of Froissart. The text shows, however, that Fabian relied mainly upon the St. Denis chronicle, which he invariably termed in his text "the frensh chronicle." Only in two places did he quote from Froissart, and then because the

St. Denis chronicle ruffled his English pride by discrediting the English troops and praising the French in two engagements. With these short extracts from Froissart, Fabian remarks in correction of the "the frensh chronicle": "but howe it was as sayeth an other wryter callyd *John Froysarde*," and again "as wytenessyth *John Froysarde*."[3]

The influence of Froissart then upon Fabian is practically nil. In spite of his efforts for picturesqueness, his work still contains much of the dull and crude method of chronicling, and though fuller in detail, is still primarily a city chronicle. To later sixteenth century historians, it proved serviceable in conveying material from the numerous London chronicles, which Fabian extensively employed. In form and style, however, it leaves much to be desired, in comparison with the treatment which Berners gave to his translation of Froissart a few years later.

Polydore Vergil

Polydore Vergil, another historian who consulted the French originals of Froissart, is one of the most interesting and one of the most maligned chroniclers of the period. He was an Italian scholar who arrived in England at the court of Henry VII in 1502. Since he had already written two books of great repute on the continent, Henry commanded him to compile a history of England. The first edition of *Historia Anglica*, written in Latin, though practically completed earlier, did not appear till 1534 at Basel. A second edition was issued in 1546 and a third with a continuation to 1538 in 1555.

As far as the reign of Edward IV, Vergil's history is a compilation. The only English authorities that he seems to have consulted are the *Brute* and Fabian, and for the

[3] Chronicles, Ellis, 1811, pp. 457 ff; 463.

relations of France and England, the histories of Froissart
and Monstrelet. There seems to be no evidence that he
knew Berners personally. In historical method, he was
more original than preceding writers, for he rarely incorporated existing narratives literally, but digested and rewrote the material in his own lucid Latin style. Moreover,
he was the first chronicler to exhibit a critical sense for
history, and his short rejection of previous English traditions made him anathema to his English rivals. His zeal
and industry is illustrated in the following:

"I first began to spend the hours of my night and day in
searching the papers of English and foreign histories. . . . I spent
six whole years . . . reading those annals and histories during
which imitating the bees which laboriously gather their honey
from every flower, I collected with discretion material proper for
a true history."

He took special pride in the fact that he was a foreigner
and could write from an objective point of view without
bias or partiality; and he modestly stated that though he
had doubtless made errors, he hoped that at least out of the
vast mass of annals "I have prepared material for others
who after me may wish to write history in a more elegant
way."

That Polydore Vergil did not have access to Berners'
translation of Froissart appears evident after considering
the dates of his compositions. In a letter to his brother
written in 1517 and published in the 1521 Basel edition of
his *De Inventoribus*, he states that he has already spent
twelve years on the *Historia Anglica,* and that it is nearing
completion. In addition we know that in 1512–24, he was
writing the reign of his patron Henry VII.[4] It is probable,
therefore, that he had finished his work on Edward III

---

[4] G. B. Churchill. Richard III up to Shakespeare. Berlin. 1900,
pp. 127–8.

and Richard II long before 1523–25, the date of Berners' Froissart.

Polydore Vergil's daring attack upon the history of Geoffrey of Monmouth and the mythical character of Brutus brought down upon his history a series of unjust attacks by contemporaries and successors. Leland characterized him as "an untrustworthy writer who mingled truth with fiction," and Sir Henry Savile called him "homo Italus, et in rebus nostris hospes." Caius accused Vergil of burning the manuscripts of ancient historians to cover his own errors, and later Gale and Wood said that he borrowed books from the University Library in Oxford which he did not return, and that he had pillaged libraries and sent a whole shipload of histories and records to Rome.[5] In spite of this abuse Vergil's history is distinguished for its classic eloquence and clarity and for its invaluable authority in matters pertaining to the reign of Henry VII.

The *Historia Anglica* had more influence upon succeeding chronicles than upon the later chronicle plays for two reasons. In the first place it was written in Latin, a language that playwrights avoided, when numerous adequate English sources were available; and in the second place though a translation of the 1546 edition exists in manuscript form, the edition of 1534 was incorporated by Grafton in 1543 and employed by succeeding English historians. Hence it found its way eventually to the dramatist, though probably through an English medium.

II

FROISSART'S CHRONICLE IN ENGLAND AFTER BERNERS' TRANSLATION, 1523–5

Nine years after Fabian's history appeared, Lord Berners

[5] Cf. Preface, Ellis, Three Books of Polydore Vergil's English History. Camden Society, Vol. XXIX, London.

gave to the English reading public the first translation of Froissart's *Chronicles.* The extent of its influence and the importance of its publication have already received comment, but a more detailed account of its immediate use by succeeding historians is of considerable aid in determining its continuous vogue.

Edward Hall

Edward Hall, the son of John Hall of Shropshire, was born in London in 1498 or 1499, and received his education first at Eton and then Cambridge. Called to the bar at Gray's Inn, he subsequently entered Parliament as a servant of the Crown. He died in 1547, the year of Henry VIII's death. Hall's *Chronicle,* entitled the *Union of the Two Noble and Illustrious Families of Lancaster and York.* was first published by Richard Grafton in 1548. Some writers state that the work was printed by Berthelet in 1542, but no such copy exists; and the evidence for such an edition rests upon the statement of Bishop Tanner in the Bibliotheca Brittanica (p. 372) and upon a copy in the Grenville Library, which contains leaves differing from the known perfect editions of 1548 and 1550. Some critics think that the many changes made in a single edition of many important works of this period, afford no reason for disbelieving that the edition issued by Grafton in 1548 was the first.[6] Whibly, however, states that the first edition of 1542 was "so effectively burnt by the orders of Queen Mary that it exists only in fragments."[7]

Whatever may be the date of the first edition, Hall's chronicle is not, as has sometimes been supposed, an entirely original work. That part preceding the reign of

[6] G. B. Churchill, Palæstra, X, p. 173.
[7] Cambr. Hist. of Eng. Lit., III, p. 359.

Henry VIII is so thoroughly different in style and treatment from the remainder as to make the chronicle two separate works. The first part, compiled from numerous authorities, relies for the reign of Henry VII upon Vergil, who is often translated literally. Certain evidences that have not yet been gathered together and published make it plausible that the history is the work of two authors, though Whibly holds the conventional opinion that with the accession of Henry VIII, Hall began "a fresh and original work."

Although the chronicle of Hall is of no particular importance for this study, since the narrative begins virtually where Froissart's concludes, namely with the death of Richard II and the coronation of Henry IV, its attitude of cheerful scepticism regarding Froissart is noteworthy. In the dedication is brought against him the charges of falsification and fabrication. Like all other succeeding chronicles, this one refers to the translation as Froissart's, not mentioning Berners; but it is probable that the writer had been reading Berners' new edition of 1542 which Middleton had just issued. The passage in the dedication referring to Froissart, reads:

"So that in fine, all the stories of the knights from Kyng Willyam the firste, to Kyng Edward the third, bee set furthe at length by diverse authours in the Latin Tongue, as by Matthewe of Paris sometyme religious, in saincte albons and other. After whome *John Frossart* wrote the lives of Kyng Edward the third, and King Richard the seconde, so compendiously and so largely, that if there were not so many thynges spoken of in his long workes, I might believe all written in his greate volumes to bee as trewe as the Gospell. But I have redde an olde Proverbe which saithe, that in many woordes, a lye or twagne sone maie scape. Sithe the ende of Frossarte whiche endeth at the begynnyng of Kyng Henry the fourthe, no man in the Englishe tounge, hath

either set furth their honors accordyng to their desertes, nor yet
declared many notable actes, worthy of memorie dooen in the
tyme of seven Kynges, whiche after Kyng Richarde suceeded.
Except Robert Fabian and one without name, which wrote the
common English chronicle. Men worthy to be praysed for ther
diligence, but farre shotyng wade from the truth of an historie."[8]

Hall's chronicle therefore did not use Froissart for the
last years of Richard II in spite of Sidney Lee's statement to the contrary. In his life of Berners,[9] Lee states
that Hall, Fabian and Holinshed were indebted to Berners.
This opinion holds true, however, only of Holinshed, for
Fabian's chronicle appeared nine years before Berners'
edition. Moreover, the criticism cited above is the only
instance of distrust of Froissart's chronicle throughout the
period; the following historians, Grafton, Holinshed, Stow
and Speed, did not hesitate to incorporate extracts from
the translation of Lord Berners.

Richard Grafton

Richard Grafton is chiefly known as the printer and
compiler of famous books of the period. He was instru-
mental in issuing several editions of Coverdale's Bible; in
1539 he printed at London *The Great Bible* and ten years
later the first Book of Common Prayer.

During the reign of Henry VIII he was printer to Prince
Edward and afterward to Edward VI and to Lady Jane
Grey. On the accession of Mary, Grafton was thrown into
prison, but after his release became, like Hall, a member of
Parliament. Grafton's first historical publication was the
first edition of Hardyng's metrical chronicle to which he
made an extensive prose continuation, and issued probably
several times with various changes in 1543. This contin-

[8] Hall's Chronicle, Ellis, London, 1809, vi.
[9] D.N.B.

uation is merely a compilation from Polydore Vergil and More's Richard III. Five years later he brought out Hall's Chronicle, to which he added material compiled, as he says, from "divers and many pamphlets and papers" that Hall had left.

He then composed and published an *Abridgement of the Chronicles of England* which was printed in 1562 and re-issued in 1563, 1564, 1570 and 1572.

But in summarizing British history Grafton had a formidable rival, and a far abler chronicler, namely John Stow, who issued in 1565 his *Summarie of English Chronicles.* To equal his rival, Grafton published in the same year an abridgment of his own *Abridgement,* entitled *A Manual of the Chronicles of England,* in which he accused Stow of plagiarizing his previous edition of 1562. He further added to the heat of the controversy by sneering "at the memories of superstitious foundacions and fables, and lyes foolishly *Stowed* together." Stow in retort spoke of the "thundering noice of empty *tonnes* and unfruitful *graftes* of Momus offspring," and in a new edition of his *Summarie of Chronicles,* 1570, he accused Grafton of falsifying both Hardynge and Hall. Grafton immediately answered in vindication of himself, and thus the warfare continued in the prefaces of successive editions of their works, until finally in 1573 Stow closed the controversy by repudiating with severity all of Grafton's historical work.

But meanwhile in 1568 Grafton had published a more ambitious history entitled *A Chronicle at Large and Meere History of the Affayres of Englande,* usually known as *Grafton's Chronicle.* A second edition appeared in the following year with a eulogy of the author by Thomas Norton.[10] On the appearance of *Grafton's Chronicle,* Stow charged his rival with patching up the work from Fabian

[10] Reprinted by Ellis. 2 vols., London, 1809.

and Hall, an accusation with more truth than fiction, for Grafton had copied literally a great many passages from Hall and supplemented them with Vergil and Fabian. In this connection, however, Grafton is for us the most important of all the chroniclers, since he was the first and only one to extract *whole pages* of Berners' Froissart and incorporate them literally in his text. He seems to have realized that Froissart's accounts of Edward III and Richard II had been neglected, and that truth demanded the inclusion of the more detailed and original stories of Froissart. Among these the principal one describing the Wat Tyler Rebellion of 1381, he introduced as follows:

"And because ye shall understand the truth thereof. . . . I have purposed fully to set foorth at length, the truth and whole discourse therof unto you, as *Froissart* doth at large write the same."[11]

In employing Berners, Grafton occasionally abridged the narrative and supplemented short extracts from Fabian, but in general left the narrative intact. How closely he follows Berners, and, not as might be contended, a French original, the parallel passages below from both chronicles testify:

Grafton, I, p. 395.	*Berners' Froissart,* I, p. 211.[12]
" Soone after by the commandment of Pope Innocent the sixt, there came into Englande the Lorde Taylleran Cardinall of Piergort; and the Lord Nicholas, Cardinall of Dargell. They treated for a peace betweene the two Kinges, but	" Anone after, by the commandement of Pope Innocent the sixt, there came into Englande, the lorde Taylleran, Cardynall of Pyergot and the lorde Nycholas, cardynall of Dargell they treated for a peace bytweene the two Kynges

11 Chronicle, 2 vols. London, 1809. I, p. 417.

12 All quotations from Berners' Froissart in this study have been taken from the reprint of E. V. Utterson. 2 vols. London, 1812.

nothing came to effect. But yet at the last a truce betweene the two Kinges and all their assistentes was concluded for to endure unto the feast of Saint John baptist, 1359, that is to say for three yeres. And out of this truce was expected the Lorde Philip of Nauerre and his alyes, the Countesse of Mountford, and the Duchie of Britaine.

Anone after, the Frenche King was remoued from the Sauoy unto the Castell of Windsore, and all his householde, and went on huntyng and hawking there at his pleasure, and the Lorde Phillip his sonne with him but all the other prisoners abode stil at London, and yet went to see the King at their pleasure, and were receyued onely upon their faythes."

but the coude bring nothing to effect, but at last by good meanes they procured a truse betwene the two Kynges and all their assysters, to endure tyll the feest of Saynt Johan the Baptyst, in the yere of our lorde God MCCCLIX and out of this truse was excepted ye Lorde Philyppe of Nauerr and his alyes, the Countesse of Mountfort, and the ducy of Bretayne.

Anone after, the french Kyng was remoued fro the Sauoy to the castell of Wyndsore, and all his householde, and went a huntyng and a haukyng ther about at his pleasur, and the lorde Philypp his son with hym; and all the other prisoners abode styll at London, and went to se the Kyng at their pleasure, and were receyued all onely on their faythes."

Ralph Holinshed

Ralph Holinshed, whose *Chronicles of England, Scotland and Ireland* appeared for the first time in 1578, is the best known chronicler of the century because of his relation to Shakespeare. In many ways one of the most industrious writers, he consulted no less than 181 authorities besides numerous books and registers. After Holinshed's death in 1580, John Hooker with the assistance of Francis Thynne,

Abraham Fleming and John Stow brought out a new edition that furnished Shakespeare and other writers with history for chronicle plays.

For the reigns of Edward III and Richard II, Holinshed took from Berners' translation many short passages, which, when taken as a whole, show that he relied on Froissart more than upon any other authority.[13] His other sources in order of importance were Walsingham, Vergil, Fabian, and Caxton, for Edward III; and Knighton, Walsingham and Fabian for Richard II.

Unlike Grafton, Holinshed preferred to abbreviate and adapt Berners' repetitious narrative to suit his own needs; but a sufficient amount of Berners' text remains to assure us that Holinshed did not consult a French original, as the following parallel passages will serve to illustrate:

Berners' Froissart, I, p. 211	*Holinshed*, III, p. 391[14]
" Anone after, by the commandment of Pope Innocent the sixt, there came into Englande, the lorde Taylleran, Cardynall of Pyergot and the lorde Nycholas, cardynall of Dargell they treated for a peace bytweene the two Kynges but at last by good meanes they procured a truse bytwene the two Kynges and all their assysters, to endure tyll the feest of Saynt Johan the Baptyst, in the yere of our lorde God MCCCLIX	" About the same time, there *came* over *into England* two cardinals, the one called *Talirand* being bishop of Alba (commonlie named the small *cardinall of Pierregot*) and the other named *Nicholas* intituled *cardinall* of S. Vitale or (as Froissard saith) *of Dargell,* they were sent from *pope innocent the sixt* to intreat *for a piece* betwixt the kings of England and France; *but they* could not *bring* their purpose

[13] Holinshed did not derive his Froissart material from Grafton, because he consulted Berners for events that Grafton did not include. For example, the secret journey of Edward III to Calais in 1349 . . . (Hol., III, pp. 378 ff.) not in Grafton (I, p. 386).

[14] Holinshed's Chronicles. London, 1587. 3 vols.

and out of this truse was excepted ye Lorde Philyppe of
Nauerr and his alyes, the Countesse of Mountfort, and the
ducy of Bretayne.

Anone after, the french Kyng
was remoued fro the Sauoy to
the castell of Wyndsore, and
all his householde, and went a
huntyng and a jaukyng ther
about at his pleasur, and the
lorde Philypp his son with hym;
and all the other prisoners
abode styll at London, and
went to se the Kyng at their
pleasure, and were receyued all
onely on their faythes."

to anie perfect conclusion, although they remained for the
space of two yeares; but yet
onlie *by good means they procured a truce betweene the said
kings and their assistan to indure* from the time of the publication thereof, unto *the feast
of S. John Baptist,* which
should be *in the year 1359; out
of* which the truce *was excepted the L. Philip of Nau-
verre and his allies, the Countess of Montfort and the whole
duchie of Britaine.*

*Anone after, the French king
was remoued from Sauoie* unto
the castell of Windsor with all
his household and then he *went*
on *hunting and hawking there-
about at his pleasure and the
lorde Philip* his sonne with him:
all the residue of the *prisoners
abode still at London* but were
suffered to go up and downe
and to come to the court when
they would."

John Stow

Acquaintance has already been made with John Stow
and his bitter altercations with his rival Richard Grafton.
Stow holds the record for the most extensive and conscientious series of historical works of all the chroniclers. He
is famous not only for his *Summarie of Englishe Chronicles,* but also for his *Annales* and his *Survey of London.*

The *Annales,* his chief claim to history in the large, first published in 1580, is excellent in chronological exactness. Camden wrote of him: "His industry is praised by all, though his judgment leaves something to seek; but his work is of such quality as to entitle him to a foremost place amongst our annalists." We also know that he was "a zealous collector of chronicles and memorials," and "an indefatigable searcher of records."[15]

Stimulated probably by his keen rivalry with Grafton, who had restored Froissart, Stow searched for other sources and brought forward the chronicles of Matthew Paris, and Thomas Walsingham. For the period 1327–1400 he relied mainly upon Walsingham and Knighton, two authentic contemporary sources. Only in three instances did he quote from Berners' translation: a paragraph concerning one, William Wicham (Annales 1631, p. 267); a passage of sixteen lines describing the battle of Otterburn (p. 267); and a description of Froissart's visit to England in 1395, and of the Irish expedition of Richard in the same year. His indebtedness to Berners for this passage is clearly evident:

Berners, II, p. 610	*Stow,* p. 310[16]
" Than I demaunded of hym the maner of the hole that is in Irelande called Saynt Patrykes purgatorie, if it were true that was sayd of it or nat. Then he sayd that of a suretie suche a hole there was, and that a knyght of Englande hadde ben there whyle the Kynge laye at Dunelyn. . . ."	" He *demaunded* of Sir William Lisle . . . *the manner of the hole that is in Ireland is called Saynt Patrikes purgatory, if it were true that was* said of it or not; who answered *that such a hole* there was and that himsele and another Knight had been there while the King lay at Dubline. . . ."

Several years later in 1598 and 1603, Stow had reference to Berners' Froissart again for his *Survey of London.* In

[15] Kingsford, Eng. Hist. Lit. in the 15th Cen., p. 266.
[16] *Annales,* London, 1631.

the description of the Tower Royall he writes "but on the 15 of June (saith Frosard) Wat Tyler being slaine, the Kyng went to this Ladie Princesse his mother, then lodged in the Tower Royall. . . ."[17] That Stow could not improve upon the style of Lord Berners is proved by the following description of the royal procession, which represents Berners at his best and which the later historian was wise enough to leave intact:

Berners Chap. CLXIX	*Stow, Survey,* II, p. 30
" So the same Sonday, about thre of the clocke at afternone, there issued out of the toure of London, first, thre score coursers apparalled for the justes, and on every one a squier of honour ridyng a softe pase. Than issued out thre score ladyes of honour mounted on fayre palfreys, ridying on the one syde, richely apparelled; and every lady ledde a knight."	" At the day appointed, there issued forth of the tower, about the third houre of the day, 60 coursers, apparalled for the Iusts, and vpon every one an Esquier of honour riding a soft pace: then came forth 60 Ladyes of honour mounted vpon palfraies, riding on the one side, richly apparelled, and every Lady led a knyght."

John Speed

John Speed is the last of the chroniclers to make extensive use of Berners' Froissart. Although he added nothing new in the way of historical facts, he wrote his chronicle in an ornate and finished style with a charm of phrasing not found in other chronicles. Moreover the form of his history is compact and well ordered; his narrative complete and adequate. That it received the commendation of Bolton, none too generous a critic of histories, is sufficient comment. His *History of Great Britaine* appeared in 1611

[17] Kingsford, Survey of London. 2 vols. I, p. 71. Cf. also p. 244.

and like the other chronicles presents a wonderful array of authorities, showing that he had the entire literature of history before him. Like the others he frequently refers in his margins to *Froissard*, although he has also digested the works of Walsingham, Vergil, Grafton, Holinshed, Stow, and others. The adoption of Berners' diction in the following passage shows that he used the English version of Froissart:

Berners, Chap. CXXVIII

" Than the Kyng caused a parlee to be made by the wode syde behynde his hoost, and ther was set all cartes and caryages, ande within the parke were all their horses, for every man was a fote . . . than the Kyng lept on a *hobby* with *a whyte rodde in his hand one of his marshals on the one hande and the other on the other hand:* "

Speed, p. 577[18]

" King Edward closed his battels at ther back . . . by felling and plashing of Trees, placing his carriages there and other impediments whatsoeuer, having commanded all men to put from them their horses, which were left among the carriages . . . Thus placed to the best advantage, King Edward visiteth the ranckes in person, riding upon a pleasant *Hobby*, hauing onely a *white rod in his hand betweene the two marshals of his fiield* . . ."

Samuel Daniel

The *History* of Samuel Daniel, which appeared a year later than Speed's *History of Britaine*, remains for consideration. *The Collection of the History of England*, Daniel's chief work in prose, gained him some fame among his friends. It extends, however, only to the end of the reign of Edward III and "heere," he says, "I leaue, unless

[18] For other references to Froissart, see Speed, pp. 95, 582, 599, 604.

by this which is done, I finde incouregement to goe on.''
Doubtless the encouragement was not forthcoming, and it
is not hard to see why. The narrative is a dull and pro-
saic catalogue of names, dates and events with no life or
color, and no insight into history, or appreciation of its
meaning. Moreover the work resembles the summaries
and epitomes of history (he calls it a Breuiary) such as
Stow and Grafton had ceaselessly issued, although, of
course, it is more extensive and pretentious. In his *Certain Advertisements to the Reader*, he gives the names of
his sources, and his reference to Froissart comes naturally
among the long list of authorities that he consulted for his
last chapters on Edward III: "*In the Liues of* Edward *the
First,* Edward *the Second and Third:* Froissart *and* Walsingham *with such Collections as by* Polydore Virgile,
Fabain, Grafton, Hall, Holingshed, Stow *and* Speed, *dili-
gent and Famous Transilors in the search of our History,
have beene made and divulged to the world.*[19]

The following table summarizes the sources of English
chronicles for the reigns of Edward III and Richard II
(1325–1400) with special reference to Berners' Froissart.

Main Sources	Minor Sources
1516 *Fabian.* Les Chroniques de St. Denys.	Polychronicon.
	Brute.
	Froissart (twice from French version).
1534 *Vergil.* Fabian.	Froissart from French version.

[19] Grosart, IV, p. 82.

1542 *Hall.* Vergil.

Polychronicon.
Fabian and others.
Traison et Mort du
    Roy Richart.

1568 *Grafton.* Berners' " Froissart."

Vergil.
Fabian.

1578 *Holinshed.* Berners' " Froissart."
Thomas Walsingham.
Fabian.
Polydore Vergil.

Knighton.
Jacob Meir.
Caxton.
Grafton (five
    times).
Stow (five times).

1580 *Stow.* Walsingham.
Knighton.

Berners' " Frois-
    sart " (three
    times).
Also employed in
    *Survey of Lon-
    don.*

1611 *Speed.* Walsingham.
Froissart.

All others.

1612 *Daniel.* Froissart and all others.

PART II

FROISSART AND THE ENGLISH CHRONICLE PLAYS

CHRONOLOGICAL OUTLINE FOR PART II

1377 Richard II ascends the throne under the protectorate of his
uncle, Duke of Gloucester (Woodstock).

1381 Wat Tyler and Jack Straw Rebellion.

1388 Richard throws off control of Gloucester.

1397 Murder of Gloucester at Calais.

1399 Deposition and murder of Richard II.

1587 *Life and Death of Jack Straw* (written?).

1589–90? *The Raigne of King Edward the Third* (written).

1591? *A Tragedy of Richard the Second* (Woodstock) (written).

1593–94 First quarto of *Jack Straw*.

1594 First four books of the *Civil Wars* S. R.

1595–7 Shakespeare's *Richard the Second* (written).

1596 First quarto of *Edward the Third*.

1597 First quarto of *Richard the Second* (Shakespeare).

1597 First edition of Drayton's *England's Heroicall Epistles*.

CHAPTER IV

THE STORY OF KING EDWARD III

The career of King Edward III is famous chiefly for his brilliant series of victories over the Scots and the French during the Hundred Years War. In history he is remembered as the father of the Black Prince, watching the brave deeds of his son at Crecy and Poitiers, but in poetry and fable King Edward is chiefly celebrated as the lover of the beautiful and virtuous Countess of Salisbury.

This famous love episode between the Countess and King Edward, originating perhaps in the gossip of Edward's court after his expedition to Scotland against David Bruce in 1341, found its way into history in the French chronicle of Jean le Bel. Froissart, who had visited England in 1361, apparently had heard the story at court in the elaborate dress that time and imagination had given it. Moreover the death of this Countess, who dared defy the King, having taken place only several years before, had doubtless caused the court to herald her fame. At any rate when Froissart began his prose history by incorporating the work of Jean le Bel, he greatly amplified the love story, and retold it with all the elaboration and detail that he knew, omitting, however, his master's gross ending.

Briefly summarized the story reads as follows. During the expedition against David Bruce, King Edward was forced to come to the relief of the Castle of Roxborough, then under siege by the Scots. Within the castle lived the Countess of Salisbury, a lady famed for her grace and beauty. Her husband, Sir William Montague, was absent on a mission to France. On entering the castle Edward, immediately overcome by the beauty of the Countess, made violent love to her. She repelled his advances, however, with such firmness, grace, and dignity that Edward, abashed and chagrined, respected her fidelity and went off to the war.

This tale, so vividly narrated by Froissart, subsequently attracted the attention of the Italian novelist Bandello. As Bandello thought this story a little too tame for Italian taste, he proceeded to make a number of notable changes and additions to heighten its dramatic effectiveness. He brought into the tale a secretary and letters between Edward and the Countess; he made the father and mother of the lady pander to the King; he killed her husband, and portrayed the Countess about to stab herself, and then begging the King to slay her; and finally made the King propose marriage, and actually marry her.

With Bandello's new amplifications and adornments, this episode passed over all modern Europe, appearing for four hundred years in varying forms in the literatures of England, France, Germany, the Netherlands, and Spain as Dr. Gustave Liebau has demonstrated in his exhaustive study of the story.[1]

We are concerned here, however, with the ramifications of the story in England in the sixteenth century. Although the episode was known in England through Berners' translation of Froissart and through Grafton's chronicle, the majority of English versions follow the story as revised by Bandello. Bandello's version came into England by way of France, for in 1559 Boisteau rendered it into French in *Les Histoires Tragiques;* and William Painter translated Boisteau's account for his *Palace of Pleasure* (1566–7).

Painter, however, introduced the story by a preface con-

[1] Litterarhistorische Forschungen, Berlin, 1900.

taining some attempted corrections that have added to the confusion of the names of the principal characters. He says:

". . . the auctour of the same perchaunce hath not rightlye touched the proper names of the aucthours of this tragedie, by perfecte appellations: as Edward the third for his eldest sonne Edward the Prince of Wales (*who as I read in Fabian*) maried the Countesse of Salesburie, which before was Countesse of Kent, and wife unto sir Thomas Holland: and whose name, (*as Polidore sayth*) was Jane, daughter to Edmond Earle of Kent, of whom the same Prince Edward begat Edward that died in his childish yeres, and Richard that afterwards was King of England the second of that name, and for that she was kin to him, was devorced; whose sayde father maried Philip, daughter to the earle of Henault, and had by her VII sonnes: and Aelips for the name of the sayde Countesse, beinge none suche amonges our vulgare termes, but *Frosard* remembreth her name to be Alice which in deede is common amonges us: and the Castell of Salesburie, where there is none by that name, uppon the frontiers of Scotlande, albeit *the same Frosard* doth make mention of a castell of the Earle of Salesburies given unto him by Edward the third when he was sir William Montague and maried the saide Lady Alice for his service and prowesse against the Scottes; and Rosamburghe for Roxboroughe: and that the said Edwarde when hee saw that hee could not by loue and other perswasions attaine the Countesse but by force, maried the same Countesse, which is altogether untrue, for that *Polydore* and other aucthors do remember but one wife that hee had, which was the sayde vertuous Queene Philip, with other like defauts. . . ."[2]

In spite of Painter's explanations Edward III, and not his son, Edward the Black Prince, was the lover of the Countess. Painter's corrections are interesting, however, as proof that he consulted the old account of the tale as told

[2] Painter, Palace of Pleasure, Jacobs. London, 1890, I, p. 336.

by Berners' Froissart. His mistakes, moreover, became stumbling blocks in the path of a later poet, who composed two verse epistles based on the *Palace of Pleasure*. This was Michael Drayton, who after versifying the episode in his *England's Heroicall Epistles*, 1595–7, reproduced in his *Notes of the Chronicle history*[3] the substance of Painter's preface. This led him also to entitle the two epistles *Edward the Blacke-Prince to Alice Countesse of Salisbury; and Alice Countesse of Salsbury to the Blacke Prince*.[4] In the *Notes* he states after Painter:

"Bandello . . . being an Italia as it is the peoples custom in that clime, rather to faile sometime in the truth of circumstance . . . thinking it to be a greater triall that a Countesse should be sude unto by a King, then by the sonne of a King, and consequently, that the honour of her chastitie should be more, hath caused it to be generally taken so; but as by *Polidore, Fabian* and *Froisard*, appeares the contrarie is true."

Again in almost the words of Painter, Drayton says:

"*. . . whose name is said to have bin Aelips; but that being rejected as a name unknowne among us, Froisard* is rather beleeued, who calleth her Alice."

This literal following of Painter seems to prove that Drayton did not independently consult Berners' Froissart.

Three other Elizabethan versions of this tale are extant: (1) *The Story of King Edward III and the Countess of Salisbury* in prose without date but published anonymously at Whitehaven. (2) *Of King Edward III and the Fair Countess of Salisbury*, a ballad (sometimes, but erroneously ascribed to Thomas Deloney), which also followed Painter's version and appeared according to Liebau after the drama

---

[3] Poems. Spenser Soc., 1888, I, pp. 225 ff; 232.

[4] See G. Liebau. König Eduard III, etc. Berlin, 1900, pp. 17 ff.

King Edward III, and hence is probably derived from it.
(3) The well known play, *The Raigne of King Edward III*,
anonymously issued in 1596.[5]

THE RAIGNE OF KING EDWARD THE THIRD

The Raigne of King Edward the Third was entered on
the Stationers' Register, and licensed for publication on
December 1, 1595. This is the first record of the existence
of the play, but no evidence has yet been discovered as to
where, when and by whom it was either written or acted.
The first quarto appeared in the following year without
signature but entitled: "The Raigne of King Edward the
Third: as it hath bin sundrie times plaied about the Citie of
London (London, Printed for Cuthbert Burby 1596)."
Three years later appeared a second anonymous quarto,
again printed for Burby, bearing the title "The Rayne of
King Edward III as it hath bene sundry times played about
the Citie of London. Imprinted at London by Simon Staf-
ford for Cuthbert Burby; and are to be sold at his shop
neere the Royall Exchange 1599." Three anonymous quartos were entered on the Stationers' Register for the years
1609, 1617, and 1625, but none of them is extant. In the
lists of transfers of copyright plays, Edward III was assigned to Welby by Mrs. Burby on October 16, 1609; on
March 2, 1617, by Welby to Snodham; on February 23,
1625, by Mrs. Snodham to W. Stansby; and on March 4,
1638, by Mrs. Stansby to Bishop. This long list of transfers, and the phrase "sundry times played" are evidence
of its popularity, while Thomas Heywood likewise refers

[5] In the first story of Pettie's *Palace of Pleasure*, entitled Camma
and Sinorix, Camma refers to Painter's version of the Countess of
Salisbury. Cf. King's Classics, Gollancz, vol. I, p. 33.

to its reception by the Elizabethan playgoers in his *Apology for Actors :*[6]

" What English prince, should hee behold the true portraiture of that famous King Edward the Third, foraging France, taking so great a king captive in his owne country, quartering the English lyons with the French flowerdelyce, and would not bee suddenly inflam'd with so royale a spectacle, being made apt and fit for the like atchievement."

In 1656 Edward III is coupled with Shakespeare's name in "an exact and perfect Catalogue of all plays that are printed" which was prefixed to Goffe's *Careless Shepherdess.* His ascription of the play to Shakespeare is rendered untrustworthy by his statement that Edward II and Edward IV were also Shakespeare's. Although the drama was listed in Langbaine's *Account of Dramatick Poets* and in other annals of plays, it was not reprinted until 1760 when Capell published his *Prolusions or Select Pieces of Ancient Poetry.* He considered it a "play thought to be writ by Shakespeare,"—an opinion based on aesthetic considerations, and on his strange notion that in 1595 there was no known writer equal to such a play. Like the majority of 18th century editors, Capell followed strictly neither quarto, but relied on his own judgment for meanings of lines. He made the first table of dramatis personae, divided the play into acts and scenes, and corrected many unintelligible passages. But an unfortunate system of editing led him to confuse not only his own text, but all succeeding issues that followed his edition. He placed a list of original readings of quartos with a number of his own conjectural readings, and succeeding editors in ignorance of this unique method accepted the whole list as original readings of the quartos. Hence the drama continued in various mutilated forms through the editions of Tieck, 1851; Delius, 1854; Collier,

[6] Shak. Soc. Pub., London, 1843. V, 15, p. 21.

1864; Moltke, 1869; and all others previous to 1886. In this year Warnke and Proescholdt discovered the mistake and issued the first reliable text.

The sources of Edward III have been frequently sought in the chronicles of Holinshed and in the *Palace of Pleasure* by William Painter. The first two acts of the drama describe Edward's expedition against the Scots, and his love for the Countess of Salisbury; the last three acts his wars with France; the sea fight at Sluys, and the brilliant victories of the Black Prince at Crecy, Calais and Poitiers.

Critics have generally asserted that the wars (I, 1; II, IV, V) came from Holinshed, and the love episode (I, 2; 120–III) from Painter's *Palace of Pleasure*. To support this opinion Warnke and Proescholdt selected passages from Holinshed with reference to the play, and discussions of sources since their edition[7] have accepted this source as final. Dr. Liebau, who has been most thorough in his valuable researches of the Countess of Salisbury story in modern literatures, has traced its literary origin to Jean le Bel and Froissart. But although he was aware of Berners' translation, he neglected like his predecessors to compare it with the play. Re-examination of the chronicle material shows that Holinshed contains nothing with reference to the play that is not set forth more fully in Froissart; and that there are scenes in the play for which Holinshed has no account, that Froissart describes in detail. One of these scenes depicts the Villiers-Salisbury story, which has long lacked a source, and which is treated by no English chronicle. Moreover, fully one half of the Countess episode itself, it is easy to demonstrate, was drawn by the dramatist directly from Froissart; while only the other half was derived from Painter. Grafton's chronicle, which, as has been noted, incorporated the Countess story from Berners'

[7] Pseudo-Shakespearian Plays, Halle, 1886.

translation, might also have supplied the material for the play, had he not, like all the English chroniclers, omitted the aforementioned Villiers-Salisbury episode (IV, 1–3). Therefore, it seems conclusive that Berners' Froissart which contains both of these episodes must have been the direct source of Edward III. The play also often resembles in a striking way the order of the chronicle narrative, as well as its details and phraseology.

It has been thought best to substantiate these statements by full quotations from Berners' Froissart, selected and arranged under references to lines of the play. To facilitate the reader, brief summaries of each act or scene are given to introduce the subject matter. The reader is urged, however, to follow the quotations from the chronicles in conjunction and comparison with the text of the play.[8]

Sources for Edward III
Act I

Scene One.

London. Embassy from France, demanding homage. Edward's claim to the throne. Defiance of Edward. Preparation for war against the Scots.

(Sc. 1, l. 1–5) (*Ber.* Chap. 25, 26.) " How the lorde syr Robert of Artoyse was chased out of the realme of Fraunce." " and in the meantyme, syr Robert, erle of Artoys, came into Inglande, dysguysed lyk a merchaunt, and the king receyned hym right joyously, and reteyned hym as one of his counsaile, . . . and syr Robert of Artoys . . . nuer ceassed day nor nyght in shewyng the kyng what ryht he had to the crowne of Fraunce."

(Sc. 1, l. 5–50) (*Ber.* Chap. 5) " Now sheweth the hystery that this Philip la Beau, kyng of France, had three sones, and a feyre doughter, Isabel married into Ingland to kyng Edward the second;

---

[8] References to the play follow the edition by Tucker-Brooke. Shakespeare Apocrypha.

and these three sonnes the eldest named Lewes . . . the second
had to name Philip the great, or the long, and the thyrd was
called Charles: and all three were kynges of Fraunce after theyr
father's disecase by ryght succession eche after other, without
having any issue male of theyr bodies lawfully begoten. So
that after the deth of Charles last kyng of the three, the twelue
piers and all the baros of Fraunce wold nat gyue the realme to
Isabell the sister . . . (Salic law) . . ., so that by these reasons
. . . (they) . . . dyd gyue the realme of France to the Lord
Philyp of Valois, nephew sometyme to Philyp la Beawe."

(Sc. 1, l. 52–66) (*Ber*. Chap. 24) " And so it was about a yere
after ye Phylip of Valoys was crowned Kyng of France, and that
all the barones and nobles of the realme had made their homage
and fealty to him, except the yong king of England who had not
done his homage for the *duchy of Guyen*."

(Sc. 1, l. 67–120) (*Ber*. Chap. 35) " How Kynge Edwarde and
all his alyes dyd defye the frenche kyng."

COUNTESS EPISODE
Act I, Scene I, line 120 to Act II

(Sc. 1, l. 120–138) (*Ber*. Chap. 76) " How the scottes besieged
a castell of therle of Salysburies."

" Than king Dauyd was couselled to drawe abacke by ye ryuer
of Tyne, and to drawe toward Carlyle; and as he went thyder-
ward, he loged that nyght besyde a castel of therle of Salysburies,
the which was well kept with men a warr: captayne thereof was
sir Wyllyam Montagu, son to therle of Salisburis suster. . . . The
next day the King of scottes comaunded that euery man sholde be
redy to assayle, and they within were redy to defende; ther was a
sore assaut, and a perylous: they might a ben sene many noble
dedes on both partes. There was within present, the noble countesse of Salysbury, who was as then reputed for the most sagest
and fayrest lady of all England: the castell parteyned to her husband therle of Sailsbury, who was taken prisoner with the earle
of Suffolke before Lyle in Flanders, as ye have heard before, and
was in prison as than in the Chatelot of Parys (cf. line 133); the
kyng of Englande gaue ye same castell to the sayd erle whan

he maryd first the sayd Lady for the prowes and gode seruyce he had done before . . . *this noble lady conforted them greatly within for by regarde of such a lady, and by her swete coforting, a man ought to be worthe two men at nede.* . . . Theye of the castell sawe well, if Kynge Dauyd cotynued his sege, how they shuld haue moche ado to defende them and their castell; wherfore they toke counsell amonge them, to send to Kyng Edward, who lay at Yorke . . . than they loked among them who shulde to the message but they coulde fynde none that wolde leaue the castell . . . than whan the captayne *Sir William Montagu* saw that, he sayd . . . I shall put my body in aduentur to do this message. . . . Thus at mydnight, Sir Wyllyam Montagu passed through thoost " . . . (slew two opposing Scots, and arriving at the camp of King Edward, delivered the message).

Ber., Chap. 73 (for the names of the besieged cities, lines 127–130) " ye haue heard here before . . . how the lordes of Scotlande had taken agayne dyuers towns and fortresses for thglysshmen, such as they helde in Scotlande . . . the citie of *Berwyke* and *Rousburge* . . . they passed nat ferre of fro Berwyke and came to the ryuer Tyne, brennyng all the country round about them and at last came to *Newcastle.* . . ."

Painter I, 342.[14] (for the name *Warwick,* father of the Countess of Salisbury.) " And after she had lamented the death of her husband . . . she returned to her father's house which was *Earl of Warwick.*"

(Sc. 1, l. 133–4) (*Ber.* Chap. 78.) " Thus there *Mountefort* conquered the country and made himself to be called the Duke of Britain. . . ."

Scene Two.

King David assures the French King that he will not parley with Edward. Edward arrives at the castle of Roxbourough and falls in love with the Countess.

(Sc. 2, l. 18–39) (*Ber.* Chap. 33.) " And the french king sent certayne messagners into Scotland, to the lordes ther, such as kept

---

[14] Palace of Pleasure, Jacobs, London, 1890.

warr agaynst theglisshmen, offryng them great ayde and confort, so yt they wolde take no peace, nor truse, with ye kyng of Englande, . . . Than the lordes of Scottlande couselled togyder, and joyously they accorded to his request and so sealed and sware with the kyng their lorde."

(Sc. 2, l. 47–93) (*Ber.* Chap. 77.) " The same day yt the scottes departed fro the sayd castell, kyng Edward came thyder, with all hist host, about noon, and came to the same place wher as the scottes had loged, and was sore displeased that he founde nat the scottes ther, for he cae thyder in such hast, ye his horse and men wer sore traueled. Than he comaunded to lodge ther that nyght, and sayd, howe he wolde go to ye castell, and the noble lady therein, for he had nat sene her sythe she was maryed before: than euery ma toke his logyng as he lyst. And assone as the kyng was unarmed, he toke a X or XII knyghtes wt hym, and went to the castell, to salute the countesse of Salisbury, and to se the maner of the assautes of the scottes, and the defence that was made agaynst them. Assone as the lady knewe of ye kynges comyng, she set opyn the gates, and cae out so richely be sene, that euery man maueyled of her beauty, and coude nat cease to regarde her noblenes with her great beauty, and the gracyous wordes and countenaunce that she made: whan she came to the kyng, she *knelyd downe to the yerth* (*cf. lines 107–8;—a detail not found in Painter*) thankyng hym of his socours, and so ledde hym into the castell, to make hym chere and honour, as she that coude ryght well do it: euery man regarded her maruelusly the hym-selfe coude nat witholde his regardyng of her, for he thought that he neuer sawe before, so noble, nor so fayre a lady: he was stryken therewith to the hert, with a sparcle of fyne loue, that endured longe after; he thought no lady in the worlde so worthy to be beloued as she. Thus they entred into the castell, hande in hande; the lady ledde hym first into the hall and after into the chabre, nobly aparelled; the kyng regarded so the lady that he was abasshed: at last he wet to a wyndo to rest hym, and so fell in a gret study: the lady went about to make chere to the lordes and knyghtes that were ther, and comaunded to dresse the hall for dyner; whan she had al deuysed and comaunded, thane she

came to the kyng with a mery chere, who was in a gret study,
(and she sayd) dere syr, (*cf. following speech with II, 1, 189–
196*) why do ye study so for, your grace nat dyspleased, it apar-
teyneth nat to you so to do: rather ye shulde make good chere and
be iuyfull, seyng ye haue chased away your enemies, who durst
nat abyde you; let other men study for the remynant: than the
kyng sayd, a, dere lady, knowe for trouthe, that syth I entred
into the castell, ther is a study coe to my mynde, so yt I can nat
chuse but to muse, nor can I nat tell what shall fall therof, put it
out of my herte I can nat: a, sir, quoth the lady, ye ought alwayes
to make good chere, to confort therwith your peple; god hath
ayded you so in your besynes, and hath gyuen you so great graces,
that ye be the moste douted and honoured prince in all christedome
and if the kyng of scottes haue done you any dyspyte or damage,
ye may well amende it whan it shall please you, as ye haue done
dyuerse tymes or this; sir, leaue musyng and come into ye hall,
if it please you, your dyner is all redy: a, fayre lady, quoth the
kyng; other thynges lyeth at my hert that ye knowe nat of; but
surely ye swete behauyng, the perfyt wysedom, the good grace,
noblenes, and exellent beauty that I se in you, hath so sore surprised my hert, yt I can nat but loue you, and without your loue
I am but deed (*cf. 211–216*) . . . than the lady sayde, a, ryght
noble prince, for goddessake mocke nor tempt me nat: I can nat
byleue that it is true that ye say, nor that so noble a prince as ye
be, wold thynke to dyshonour me, and my lorde, my husbande,
who is so valyant a knight, and hath done your grace so gode
seruyce, and as yet lyethe in prison for your quarell; certely sir,
ye shulde in this case haue but a small prayse, and nothing the
better therby: I had neuer as yet such a thought in my hert, nor
I trust in god neuer shall haue, for no man lyueng; (*cf. 216–276*)
if I had any suche intencyon, your grace ought nat all onely to
blame me, but also to punysshe my body, ye and by true iustice
to be dismebred; therwith the lady departed from the kyng, and
went into the hall to hast the dyner, than she returned agayne to
the kyng, and broght some of his knyghtes with her, and sayd,
sir, yf it please you to come into the hall, your knightes abideth
for you to wasshe, ye haue been to long fastyng. Than ye kyng

went into the hall and wassht, and sat down amonge his lordes,
and the lady also; the kyng etc. but lytell, he cast his eyen upon
the lady: of his sadness his knyghtes had maruell, for he was not
acustomed so to be; some thought it was bycause the scottes were
scaped from hym. All yt day the kyng taryed ther, and wyst nat
what to do; sotyme he ymagined yt honour and trouth defeded him
to set his hert in such a case, to dyshonour such a lady, and so
true a knyght as her husband was, who had alwayes well and
truely serued hym. On thother part, loue so constrayned hym,
that the power therof surmounted honour and trouth: *thus ye
kyng debated in hymself all that day, and all that night; in the
mornyng he arose and dysloged all his hoost and drewe after the
scottes, to chase them out of his realme."*

COUNTESS EPISODE (continued)

Act II

SCENE ONE.

The dramatist drew from Painter's *Palace of Pleasure*[15]
the chief events of Act II, scene 1:—King Edward's letter
to the Countess; his conference with the Countess and her
father, Warwick; Warwick's conference with his daughter;
and the following "dagger" scene. Although details of
the scenes between Edward and the Countess may well be
derived from either Berners or Painter, there is abundant
evidence to show that the author constantly referred to
Berners, e. g., the kneeling of the Countess before the King.

SCENE TWO.

The Emperor of Almaigne appoints Edward III lieuten-
ant general.

(Sc. 2, l. 1–38) (*Ber.* Chap. 32.) . "Than it was ordayned, that
the Marques of Jullers shulde go to themperour (of Almaigne) ...
the Marques and his copany foude the emperour at Florebetche,
and shewed hym the cause of their commyng ... And themperour

[15] Palace of Pleasure, Vol. I.

gaue commyssion to four knyghts, and to tuo doctours of his counsell, to make kyng Edwarde of Englande his vycarre generall throughout all the empyre. And thereof these sayd lordes hadde instrumentes publyke: confyrmed and sealed suffyciently by the emperour."

The remaining lines 39–199 of scene 2, Act II, contain the above-mentioned dagger episode, derived from Painter. In addition to several other parts of Painter's story, which the dramatist ignored, is the conclusion portraying the marriage of the King and the Countess. Edward's departure for the wars, as described by Froissart, therefore, is the ending which the dramatist employed.

Ber., Chap. 77. "Than he took leaue of the lady, sayeing my dere lady to god I comende you tyll I returne agayne: Noble prince quoth the lady: god ye father glorious be your coduct, and put you out of all vylayne thoughts sir I am & euer shalbe redy to do your grace seruyce to your honour and to myne, therwith the kyng depted." (Chap. 50) "Now . . . ye kyng of England . . . was on ye see to the intent to arryue in *Flaunders* and so into Heynalt to make ware agaynst the frechmen."

Before leaving the story of King Edward's love for the Countess as given by Lord Berners, we shall find it well to consider the theories of authorship that have been advanced for the play on account of this episode. Since the love affair is highly colored and seems to interrupt the main course of Edward's wars against the Scots and French, many critics have asserted that it must, therefore, be a later interpolation thrust into the play by some dramatist of remarkable ability. These critics with their various theories may conveniently be placed in three classes:

1. Those who believe that Shakespeare wrote the entire play. To this class belong Tieck, Capell, Collier, Teetgen, Ulrici[10] and Hopkinson—none of whom offer reasons other

[10] Ulrici retracted this opinion after reading the play in an English version.

than conjectural in support of Shakespeare's authorship; and these in absence of other evidence are untrustworthy.

2. Those believing that an early play, Edward III, was revised by Shakespeare who added the Countess episode; or that Shakespeare at least had a hand in the play. To this class belong Tyrell, Von Vincke, Hallilwell-Phillips, Tennyson, Fleay, Ward, Brandes, G. C. Moore-Smith and Schelling.

Fleay is the only member of this second class to offer evidence of Shakespeare's authorship. He has constructed with his customary ingenuity the following bit of external evidence. Edward III he says was written by Marlowe about 1589, and was acted in 1590;—dates however which are purely conjectural, but reasonable guesses. He next states that the play was revised by Shakespeare who inserted the Countess episode, and was acted in this form by Lord Strange's men in 1594 after May 9.[11] This date Fleay endeavors to establish by quoting three coincidences between lines of the play and other lines of Shakespeare's known work: (1) The phrase "their scarlet ornaments" which occurs in II, 1, 10, and in Shakespeare's sonnet 142, line 6; (2) the line "Lillies that fester smell far worse than weeds," appearing in II, 1, 451 and in Shakespeare's sonnet 94, line 14. As the sonnets were at that date (1594) still unpublished, Fleay argues that only Shakespeare could have made these repetitions. But Meres states in his Palladis Tamia (1598) that Shakespeare's "sugred Sonnets" had been circulated "among his private friends," and this fact renders such evidence untrustworthy. That the date of the play must have been after May 9 in 1594, he maintains by the third coincidence, namely the following allusion in Act II, Sc. 2, 194–197 to Shakespeare's "Rape of Lucrece," which was entered in the S. R. on that day:

11 Life of Shakespeare, pp. 119–120.

> " Arise, true English Ladie; whom our Ile
> May better boast than ever Romaine might
> Of her, whose ransact treasurie hath taskt
> The vaine indeavor of so many pens."

The four lines quoted may, or may not refer to Shakespeare's Lucrece; Shakespeare may, or may not have called his work the vain endeavor of his pen. Such vague external evidence can hardly be considered as proof either of the date, or of the revision of an old version of the play.

For proof of the existence of an old version of Edward III written by Marlowe, Fleay offers the following argument:

" In the Address prefixed to Greene's Menaphon, in a passage in which Nash has been satirising Kyd and another as void of scholarship and unable to read Seneca in the original, he suddenly attacks Marlowe, whom he has previously held up as the object of their imitation and asks what they can have of him? In Nash's own words, ' what can be hoped of those that thrust Elysium into Hell and have not learned, so long as they have lived in the spheres, the just measure of the Horizon without an hexameter?' Marlowe in I Tamburlaine v. 2 has confounded Hell in Elysium, and in Edward III horizon is pronounced hórizon. . . ."

But Mr. F. S. Boas has shown[12] that this satirical passage applies throughout to Kyd (not in the least to Marlowe), because the references of "thrusting Elysium into Hell" and "the just measure of Hórizon without an hexameter" refer to Kyd's adaptation from Virgil of the description of the lower world for his Spanish Tragedy.

To quote another of Fleay's passages in support of Marlowe's authorship:

" In Greene's Never Too Late we find Tully addressing the player Roscius, who certainly represents R. Wilson, in the words:

[12] Introduction to Edition of Kyd, XXIX.

' Why, Roscius, are thou proud with Aesop's crow, being pranked with the glory of other's feathers? Of thyself thou canst say nothing: and if the Cobbler hath taught thee to say ' Ave Caesar,' disdain not thy tutor because thou pratest in a King's chamber.' Unless another play can be produced with ' Ave Caesar ' in it, this must be held to allude to Edward III., in which play Wilson must have acted the Prince of Wales (Act I, 1, 164). The ' Cobbler ' alludes to Marlowe as a Shoemaker's son."

This evidence is too indefinite to be given great weight, because it is based upon three suppositions:

1. That "Ave Caesar" occurs in no other play.

2. That Roscius is R. Wilson.

3. That the cobbler refers to Marlowe. Granted that Roscius is R. Wilson, is it not more likely that the Cobbler refers to Wilson's Cobbler's Prophecy (before 1593, 1594) rather than to Marlowe?

To support his theory that Shakespeare added the Countess episode (1, 2, 90; II)[13] Fleay offers the following word and metrical tests: In this episode the proportion of rhyme lines to verse lines is one to seven; in other parts of the play one to twenty;—in the episode, the proportion of lines with double endings to verse lines is one to ten, in the rest of the play it is one to twenty-five. The following table taken from Warnke and Proescholdt's discussion of this question shows that this test is insufficient:

As these editors state, it is true that, as Fleay contends, "the total sum of rhymes is greater in the episode than in the principal play. (Proportion of verse lines to rhyme lines in the episode one to nine, in the other parts of the play one to twenty.) But at the same time we find that comparatively speaking some scenes of the principal play are almost as rich in rhymes as the episode (I, 1; IV, 5 and 9) and what is more surprising, that the supposed author of the

[13] Shakespeare Manual, pp. 303–306.

Act and Scene	Verse Lines	Rhyme Lines	Lines with Double Endings	
I 1	169	10	6	
I 2	166	50	11	Countess
II 1	459	36	56	Episode.
II 2	212	8	21	
III 1	189	10	3	
III 2	75	6	3	
III 3	228	6	5	
III 4	13	1	—	
III 5	115	2	1	
IV 1	43	—	6	
IV 2	85	4	4	
IV 3	85	2	6	
IV 4	161	2	15	
IV 5	127	10	9	
IV 6	17	1	1	
IV 7	35	—	5	
IV 8	10	1	1	
IV 9	64	8	3	
V	243	4	4	

episode whilst studying I, 2 and II, 1 with a great number of rhymes, should have all but rejected rhyme lines in II, 2, which has 8 rhyme lines in 212 verse lines; whereas the next following scene II, 1 exhibits ten rhymes in 189 verse lines. The most surprising figure in the rhyme test is I, 2 (50 rhyme lines; 166 verse lines) and this figure will easily be accounted for, if we remember that the last part of the scene in which the Countess engages the King to stay at her castle is wholly written in rhyme lines.

"Almost the same remarks apply to the lines with double endings. They are more frequent in the episode (88), but they are by no means wanting in the rest of the play (72). So IV, 5 is as rich in lines with double endings as I, 2 and IV, 4 is as rich as II, 2."

Moreover, the word test proves as insufficient. Fleay's word test consists of "horizon" (Act V, Sc. 1); "Ave

Caesar" (Act I, Sc. 1); "whinyards" (Act 1, Sc. 2); "Bayard" (Act III, Sc. 1); "Nemesis" (Act III, Sc. 1); "Martialist" (Act III, Sc. 3); "plate," in the Spanish sense of silver (Act I, Sc. 2; Act IV, Sc. 4); "solitariness" (Act III, Sc. 2); "quadrant" (Act V, Sc. 7); "Ure" (Act I, Sc. 1), all words foreign to Shakespeare's vocabulary.

If Fleay, as Warnke and Proescholdt show, had applied his test to the Countess scenes themselves, he would have found many words such as "decline" (I, 2, 104); "oriental" (II, 1, 11); "persuasive" (II, 1, 54); "to sot" (II, 1, 81); "to fly" (transitive) (II, 1, 87); "summer-leaking" (II, 1, 107); "Flankers" (II, 1, 185) and others such as "wantonness" that are equally un-Shakespearian.

In spite of these unreliable evidences of double authorship, the theory has been recently advanced on a little different ground by F. W. Moorman in the *Cambridge History of Literature*. He does not, like previous critics, believe the Countess episode to be "extraneous matter foisted into the play," but thinks that "on other and more substantial grounds" Shakespeare's revision of it must still be held. As evidence, however, he accepts Fleay's erroneous word and metrical tests, then assumes by conjecture the existence of a pre-Edward III play. After wavering between collaboration and revision, he finally states his belief that because the countess episode is so much superior in character and in general treatment to the rest of the play, Shakespeare must have withdrawn entirely the old rendering of it and substituted the "pearl of great price which now lies embedded in the old chronicle play."

3. The third theory of authorship maintains that Shakespeare had nothing to do with the play. To this class belong Stevens, Delius, Knight, Von Friesen, Warnke and Proescholdt, Liebau, Furnivall, Symonds, Saintsbury, Swinburne, Rolfe and Tucker-Brooke. These critics believe that

the play as a whole has never been authoritatively attributed to Shakespeare and is by no means up to his level; there is an absence of comedy, and a general lack of characterization—all the characters, high and low, from the countrymen and citizens to the King and Countess, speak the same stilted Marlowesque eloquence—nor is the episode so supremely elevated and excellent as to seem out of keeping with the rest of the play.

An additional argument against the double authorship theory is disclosed by reviewing the Countess episode as it stands in relation to the sources from which the play was derived, for a comparison seems to demonstrate that the drama was written by a single author. As has already been stated, the source of three acts of the play is derived not from Holinshed, but from Berners' Froissart. A later dramatist then did not, as has been contended, take the whole Countess episode of Painter and thrust it into an earlier Edward III. The author finding the Countess episode in the same position in Froissart's history that the dramatic version now holds in the play, merely followed the order of events that Froissart had prescribed. To fill out the episode, however, the writer selected from Painter the few details that make up the first scene of the second act and heighten its dramatic effectiveness. To render this fusion of Froissart and Painter's versions of the story clear and explicit in their relation to the drama, the following table is appended.

COUNTESS EPISODE
(not found in Holinshed)
Act I, Sc. 2, lines 120 to Act III
Froissart (1373)

Bandello, *1554*

Boisteau, *1559*

Berners' Froissart, 1523–25.   Painter, *1567*

Act I, Sc. 1

Cf. lines 121–131 with Berners, Chap. 76, 73.	Sir William Montague. Siege of the cities, Berwick, etc.	
lines 133, 134, Ber. I, Chap. 68.	Planting of Lord Mouneford in Brittayne.	line 132, Warwick as father of the Countess (Painter, Vol. I, p. 342).
lines 135–169, Ber. I, Chap. 52.	Expeditions of embassies and the gathering of allies.	

Act I, Sc. 2

lines 1–18, Ber. I, Chap. 76.	Siege of the Castle of Salisbury by the Scots under King David at Roxborough.
lines 18–39, Ber. I, Chap. 33.	League of France and Scotland.
lines 40–93, Ber. I, Chap. 77.	Flight of the Scots at the arrival of Edward.
lines 94–166, Ber. I, Chap. 77.	Meeting of King Edward and the Countess of Salisbury.

Act II, Sc. 1

		lines 1–183, I, 343–34.	Edward sends a letter to the Countess.
		lines 183–292, I, 238, 342.	Meeting of King Edward and the Countess.
		lines 293–346, I, 344–353.	The King confers with Warwick, father of the Countess.
		lines 347–459, I, 353–355.	Conference of Warwick and his daughter.

Act II, Sc. 2

lines 1–38, Ber. I, Chap. 32.	Emperor of Almaigne joins King Edward.		
lines 200–211, Ber. I, Chap. 67.	Countess remains a true wife and repulses the King's suit. King Edward returns to war.	lines 39–199, I, 359–362.	Feigned consent of the Countess and the following "dagger" scene.

According to Painter's version, King Edward, overwhelmed with admiration for the Countess immediately proposes honorable marriage, and the story closes with the tinkling of marriage bells. The playwright, however, rejected this perversion of history for which Bandello was originally responsible, and adopted Froissart's account of Edward's return to battle.

It is difficult to believe in view of this complicated fusion of Froissart and Painter that the double authorship theory has a valid argument in its favor. It seems very improbable that Shakespeare, as Fleay states, or any other dramatist could have inserted the Countess episode into an old Edward III play; nor have we any evidence for collaboration or

revision. The quotations from the sources seem to prove
that the entire play was written by a single author at one
time. Further evidence supporting this opinion and
ruining Moorman's revision theory is found in two passages in Act III which refer to the love story of the first two
acts. If a second playwright added, or revised the Countess
story, then he also must have inserted these lines in Act III.

Act III, Sc. 3, 155–7.

> "For what's his Edward but a belly god
> A tender and lasciuious wantoness
> That thother daie was almost dead for love?"

Act III, Sc. 5, 100–3.

> "Now John of France I hope,
> Thou knowest King Edward for no wantonesse
> No love sick cockney. . . ."

As far as the question of authorhip is concerned, Edward
III has never been attributed to Shakespeare except on conjectural grounds; and no reliable external, or internal evidence has been discovered to support such a view. Finally,
as the author of Edward II derived his story from Froissart, not from Holinshed, it is likely that Shakespeare had
nothing to do with the play, for, so far as is known, Shakespeare never consulted Froissart for chronicle history.

Act III

King John of France welcomes his ally, the King of
Bohemia. A mariner describes the sea fight at Sluys. De-
fiant meeting of English and French forces. Knighting of
the Black Prince, and his feats of valor in the ensuing
battles.

SCENE ONE.

(l. 1–61) (*Ber.* Chap. 123.) The french kyng . . . had sent
letters to his frendes in thempyre, to such as wer farthest of, and

also to the gentyll kyng of Behayne," (chap. 125) "and at saynt
Deuyse were redy coe the kynge of Behayne . . . the duke of
Larayne, . . . and many other great lordes and knyghtes, redy to
serve the frenche kynge."

Ber., 50.   This chapter contains a detailed account of the battle
of Sluys.   (cf. l. 6–189.)

SCENE TWO.

(l. 45–76) (*Ber.* Chap. 122.)   "and also he ordayned thre
batyls, one to go on his right hande, closyng to the see syde and
the other on his lyfte hande, and the kynge hymselfe in the
myddes, . . . Thus they sette forth . . . in this manner they brent
many other townes in that country."

SCENE THREE.

(l. 1–10) (*Ber.* Chap. 126.)   ". . . ther was a varlet called Gobyn
a Grace, who stept forthe and sayde to the kyng, sir, I promyse
you on the ieopardy of my head, I shall bringe you to suche a
place where as ye and all your hoost shall passe the ruyer of
Some without paryll, . . ." (Chap. 127) "The kynge of Englande whan he was past the ruyer . . . called Gobyn a Grace,
and dyd quyte hym his ransome . . . and gaue hym a hundred
nobles and a good horse."

(l. 18–45) (*Ber.* Chap. 122.)   ". . . after the towne of Harflewe
was thus taken and robbed without brennyng . . . they came to a
great towne well closed, called Quaretyne."   (Carentigne) Lowe
and other cities are plundered in this chapter.

SCENE FOUR.

Ber. Chap. 130.   "Of the batayle of Cressy bytwene the kyng
of England the french kyng . . . there were of the genowayes crosbowes, about a fiftene thousand, but they were so wery of goyng
a fote that day . . . whan the genowayes felte the arowes . . .
many of them cast downe their crosbowes, and dyde cutte their
strynges and retourned dysconfited."

SCENE FIVE.

(l. 1–60) (*Ber.* Chap. 130.)   ". . . and they . . . sent a messan-
ger to the kynge, who was on a lytell wyndmyll hyll; than the

knyght sayd to the kyng, sir, therle of Warwyke, . . . and other, suche as be about the prince your sonne, are feersly fought with all, . . . wherfore they desyre you, that you and your batayle wolle come and ayde them, for if the frenchmen encrease, . . . your sonne and they shall haue moche ado. Than the kynge sayde, is my sonne deed or hurt, or on the yerthe felled; no sir, quoth the knyght, but he is hardely matched, wherfore he hathe nede of your ayde. Well, sayde the kyng, retourne to him and to them that sent you hyther, and say to them, that they sende no more to me for any aduenture that falleth, as long as my soone is alyue; and also say to the, that they they suffre hym this day to wynne his spurres."

(1. 61–86) (*Ber*. Chap. 131.) ". . . than he went with all his batayle to his sonne the prince, and enbrased hym in his armes, and kyst hym . . .: the prince inclyned himselfe to the yerthe, honouryng the kyng his father."

(1. 95–114) (*Ber*. Chap. 131.) ". . .: they made iust report of that they had sens, and sayde, howe ther were XI great princes deed, fourscore baners, XII C. knightes and mo than XXX. thousande other."

Act IV

Villiers-Salisbury episode. King Edward receives beggars from Calais. News arrives that David of Scotland is a prisoner of the Queen of England. Battle of Poitiers. Victory of the Black Prince.

Villiers-Salisbury Episode	Act IV	sc. 1, 19–143
		sc. 3, 1–56
		sc. 5, 55–126

Warnke and Proescholdt found no source for the Villiers-Salisbury episode in Holinshed. G. Liebau and C. F. Tucker-Brooke state that it is found neither in Holinshed, nor in Froissart. The following quotation from Berners, chapter 135, however, gives the complete story, overlooked before because the names *Gaultier of Manny* and *a knight*

of Normandy were changed in the play to *Salisbury* and
Villiers respectively.

"It was nat long after, but that Sir Gaultier of Many fell in
communycation with a Knyght of Normandy who was his prisoner, and demaunded of hym what money he wolde pay for his
ransome; the Knight answered and sayd, he wolde gladly pay
three M crownes; well quoth the lorde Gaultyer. I knowe well
ye be kynne to the Duke of Normandy, and well beloved with
him, that I am sure, and if I would sore oppresse you, I am sure
ye wolde gladly pay X thousand crownes, but I shall deale other-
wyse with you. Woll trust you on your faythe and promise; ye
shall go to the duke your lorde, and by your means gette a save
conduct for me, and XX other of my copany to ryde through
France to Calys, payeng curtesly for all our expenses; and if you
can get this of the duke, or the Kynge my maister, nor I wyll lye
but one nyght in a place, tyll I coe there; and if ye can nat do
this, retourne agyn hyder within a moneth and yelde yourseld styll
as my prisoner. . . . The Knyght was content, and so went to
Paris to the duke his lorde, and he obtayned this passport for sir
Gaultier of M'anny and XX horse with hin all onely . . . and ther
he quyted the Knyght Norman of his ransome. Than anone after,
sir Gaultier toke his way, and XX horse with hym, and so rode
through Auuergne and when he taryed in any place, he shewed
his letter, and so was lette passe, but whan he came to Orleaunce
for all his letter, he was arrested, and brought to Parys, and there
put in prison in the Chatlet; whan the duke of Normandy knewe
thereof, he went to the Kynge his father, and shewed him how sir
Gaultier of Normandy had his save conduct wherefore he requyred
the Kynge, as moche as he might, to delyuer him, or else it shulde
be sayd, howe he had betrayd hym: the King answered and sayd,
howe he shulde be put to dethe, for he reputed hym for his great
enemy; than sayd the duke, sir if ye do so, surely I shall neuer
bere armour agaynst the Kynge of Englande nor all such as I may
let; and at his departyne, he sayd, that he wolde never entre
agayn into the Kynges host; thus the mater stode a certayne tyme.
There was a Knyght of Heynalt called Sir Mansart de Sue; he

purchased all that he myght to helpe Sir Walter of Manny, and went often in and out to the duke of Normandy; finally the Kynge was so counselled, that he was delyuered out of prison and all his cost payd—Thane he (Sir Walter) toke his leaue and departed, and rode so long by his journeys that he came into Heynalt and—so from thens he went to Cales, and was welcome to the Kynge."

SCENE TWO.

(l. 7–35) (*Ber.* Chap. 133.) " Howe the kyng of Englande layd siege to Calys and howe all the poore people were put out of the towne." " Whan the capten of Calys sawe that maner of thorder of thegleyssh men : than he constrayned all poore & meane peple to issue out of the towne . . . and as they passed through ye hoost they were demaunded why they depted & they . . . sayde bycause they had nothyng to lyue on. Than the kyng dyd them that grace . . and gaue them mete and drinke to dyner and euery pson ii d sterlyng almes. . . ."

(l. 36–60) (*Ber.* Chap. 139.) "When the quene of Englande . . . it was shewed her howe the kyng of scotts was taken by a squyer called John Coplande. . . . Than the quene wrote to the squyer comaundyng hym to bring his prisoner . . . Johan Coplande . . . answered and sayd, that as for the kyng of scottes his prisoner he wolde not delyuer hym to no ma nor woman lyueing, but all onely to the kynge of Englande his soueragne lorde. . . . Than the kyng sende incotynent to Johan Coplande, that he shulde come ouer the see to hym to the siege before Calays."

(l. 61–85) (*Ber.* Chap. 146.) " Than the kynge sayde . . . sir Gaultyer of Manny ye shall goo and say to the capytayne . . . that they lette six of the chiefe burgesses of the Towne come out bare heeded, bare foted, and bare legged, and in their shertes with haulters about their neckes, with the keyes of the towne and castell in their handes, and lette theym six yelde themselfe to my wyll."

SCENE FOUR.

Ber. Chap., 161. " That sonday all the day of cardynall traueyled in ridynge fro the one hoose to the other gladly to agree them ; but the frenche kynge wolde nat agree without he myght haue foure of the princypallist of the englysshmen at his pleasure, and the prince and all the other to yelde themselfe simply, howe beit there were many great offers made . . . the uttermost that he (the French king) wolde do was that the prince and a C. of his knyghtes shoude yelde them selfe into the kynges prison, other-wyse he wolde nat; the whiche the prince wolde in no wyse agre unto."

Scene Five.

(l. 1–55) (*Ber.* Chap. 130.) " Also the same reason there fell a great rayne and a clyps, with a terryble thouder, and before the rayne there came fleyng ouer bothe batayls a great nombre of crowes, for feare of the tempest comynge. Than anone the eyre beganne to wave clere, and the sonne to shyne fayre and bright; the which was right in the frenchmens eyen, and on the englyssh-mens backes."

Scene Six.

Ber., 162. " The lorde James Audeley . . . was in the front of that batell and there dyd maruels in armes."

Scene Seven.

Ber., 162. " On the frenche partie kynge Johan was that day a full right good knyght; if the fourth part of his menne hadde done their deuoyers as well as he dydde, the journey hadde bene his, by all lykelyhode. Howe be it they were all slayne and takenne that were there; excepte a fewe that saued themselfe that were with the kynge."

Scene Eight.

Ber., 165. " than the prince demaunded of the knyghtes that were aboute hym for the lord Audeley yf any knewe any thing of hym. Some knygtes . . . answer . . . sir he is sore hurt and lyeth in a lytter here besyde. . . ."

Scene Nine.

(l. 1–17) (*Ber.* Chap. 164.) " Howe kyng John was taken pris-oner at the batayle of Poycters."

(l. 18–64) (*Ber.* Chap. 165.) " than he (the prince) called eyght of his seruantes, and caused them to bere hym (Audeley) in his lytter to the place were as the prince was. Than the prince tooke

hym in his armes and kyst hym and made hym great chere (and
sayd) sir James . . . to thyntent to furnysshe you the better
to pursue ye warres I retayne you for euer to be my knight with
fyue hundred markes of yerely reuenewes. . . ." *Chap. 167.*
" Whan sir James Audeley was brought to his logynge, . . . he
sayd to the sayd lordes, sirs it hath pleased me lorde the prince to
gyue me fyue hundred markes of reuenewes. . . . Sirs beholde
here these foure squyers . . . I gye and resigne into their handes
the gyft . . . of fyue hundred markes . . . to them and to their
heyres foreuer."

Act V

Citizens from Calais come to Edward to sue for peace. John
Copeland, obeying Edward's order, comes to France with his
prisoner, David, King of Scotland. The Black Prince embarks
for England with King John of France as captive.

(1. 1–5; 64–96) (*Ber.* Chap. 139.) " . . . than the same John (Coplande) dyd putte his prisoner in saue kepynge, in a stronge castell, and so rode through England, tyll he cae to Douer, and there
toke the see and arryued before Calays. Whan the kyng of Englande sawe the squyer, he toke hym by the hande, and sayde . . .:
ye shall retourne agayne home . . . and thane my pleasure is,
that (ye) delyuer your prisoner to ye quene my wyfe, and in a
rewarde I assigne you nere to your house, . . . fyue hundred
pounde steryling of yerely rent, . . . and here I make you squyer
for my body." . . . " Thane . . . He presented the Kyng of
Scottes to ye quene and excused hym so largely, that the quene
and her counsell were content. Than the quene . . . tooke the see,
. . . arryued before Calays, thre dayes before the feest of Al
sayntes."

(1. 8–63) (*Ber.* Chap. 146.) " Thane the barryers were opyned,
the sixe burgesses went towardes the kyng, . . . they kneled
downe, and helde vp their handes and sayd . . . we submyt oure
self clerely into your wyll and pleasure, to saue the resydue of
the people of Calays, . . . Sir, we beseche your grace to haue
mercy and pytie on vs through your hygh nobles: than all the
erles and barownes . . . wept for pytie. Than (the kyng) com-

auded their heedes to be stryken of: than euery man requyred the
kyng for mercy but he wolde here no ma in that behalfe: . . .
Than the quene . . . kneled down and sore wepyng, sayd, a
getyll sir . . . now I hubly requyre you . . . for the love of me,
yt ye woll take mercy of these sixe burgesses. The kyng . . .
sayd, a dame, I wolde ye had ben as nowe in soe other place, ye
make such request to me yt I can nat deny you. . . ."

(l. 97–243) (*Ber.* Chap. 173.) ". . .: the same wynter ye prince
of Wales, . . . ordayned for shyppes, to conuey the frenche kyng
and his sonne, and all other prisoners into Englande."

The preceding quotations from Froissart provide a complete historical source for King Edward III, including
many essentials that are wanting in the chronicles of Grafton and Holinshed. In the second act, as has been noted,
the author of the play departed from Froissart's narrative
of the Countess episode, and adopted parts of Painter's
Palace of Pleasure. This fact with other considerations
go far as evidence that the play was written by a single
author at a single time. Since the dramatist's departures
from Berners' Froissart are few and insignificant, we may,
perhaps, be justified in calling Edward III a dramatized
and versified chronicle. Finally, certain resemblances in
phraseology would seem to show that the playwright had
the first volume of Berners' Froissart open before him while
writing the play.

CHAPTER V

THE STORY OF KING RICHARD II

To playwrights who aspired to write tragedy, the life and death of Richard II offered a more fruitful field than that of his grandfather, Edward III. The portrayal on the stage of Edward's victories in the Hundred Years war might well inspire an audience with renewed patriotism for England and St. George, as Thomas Heywood's remark has confirmed; but it could hardly arouse its deeper emotions of sympathy, pity and terror, in comparison with the sad picture of the vacillating and inglorious Richard. Perhaps this is one reason why there remain from the welter of historical literature only one play on Edward III, and three extant plays and one epic poem on the life of Richard II. Moreover, even earlier in the century, before the chronicle plays, his tragic fate had been pictured in the *Mirror for Magistrates.*

In that part of this notable work, conducted by William Baldwin,[1] four poems rehearse the fates of the four tragic heroes implicated in Richard's career and downfall. The picture of the luckless Tresilian, one of Richard's early notorious favorites, was drawn by Ferrers, who also portrayed the life and murder of the Duke of Gloucester, and the fate of his nephew, King Richard; and Chaloner was responsible for the story of Thomas Mowbray, Duke of Norfolk.

Contrary to the usual custom in composing historical poems or plays, the writers of this series make reference to

[1] Haslewood, II. London, 1870.

93

the sources from which they derived their information. Though consulting evidently a number of different accounts, they express in the link passage connecting the poems on *Northfolke* and *Richard* the following comment:

"His tragicall example of all the company we liked, howbee it a doubt was found therein, and that by meanes of the diversity of the chronicles; for whereas *Hall* (whose chronicles in this worke wee chiefly followed) maketh Mowbray appellant and Bolinbroke defendant, *Fabian* reporteth the matter quite contraryly."

A comparison of the poems with Fabian and Hall reveals how closely the authors of the poems followed these chronicles: and there are no evidences that they consulted Berners' Froissart, which differs greatly in detail, and which Hall had earlier refused to make use of.

When the London stage began in 1590 to call for chronicle history plays, interest in Richard II revived. The vicissitudes of his reign of twenty-two years, his final deposition and murder, admirably suited the Elizabethan conception of tragedy. Here was a youthful king of weak will and poor judgment, but of good intentions and attractive personality, whose vacillations in desperate circumstances drove him from high estate to ignominy, imprisonment and death. He was ever the victim on the one hand of fawning sycophants and flatterers, and on the other, of seditious relatives, who were constantly plotting his ruin. The three most notable events of his reign are his courageous dispersal of the Wat Tyler rabble in the early years; his crafty scheme to dispose of his dangerous uncle, Thomas of Woodstock, Duke of Gloucester; and his ignominious deposition and death by the contrivance of his cousin Henry of Herford (Duke of Lancaster, or Bolingbroke). Skillful dramatists of the eighties or nineties might easily make a play out of any one, or all of these events; and in the Richard II literature recorded, hardly an event in his career escaped portrayal by some poet or dramatist.

Moreover, the picture of Richard II given to the Elizabethan public by means of these several versions was in the majority of instances that which Froissart had conceived in his original and picturesque narratives; and it is partly because of his effective treatment of the beginning of the Civil Wars that his chronicle was continually used by Elizabethan poets and dramatists. In view of this fact, it will perhaps be well in preparation for special treatment of each version in relation with the chronicle, to enumerate the extant and non-extant works, and to witness the effect that the fate of Richard thus produced upon the political movements of the time.

At the Globe Theatre, April 30, 1611, Dr. Simon Forman says he witnessed a play depicting the Jack Straw Rebellion, the conspiracy of the Lords against Richard's favorite, Duke of Ireland, the murder of Gloucester, and John of Gaunt's conspiracy to place on the throne his son Henry of Herford. No play, however, covering this whole series of events remains extant, but three plays dealing with the episodes separately are all accessible.

The early years of Richard II are portrayed in the anonymous *Life and Death of Jack Straw,* written perhaps as early as 1587. The play, though crudely constructed, presents a graphic picture of the Wat Tyler Rebellion as the playwright had read it in Grafton's chronicle.[2]

A few years later another anonymous play appeared entitled *"A Tragedy of King Richard the Second, concluding the Murder of the Duke of Gloucester at Calais."* This play written perhaps in 1591 and sometimes called *Woodstock,* is unique in its daring elevation of the seditious

2 See Chapter VI.

Gloucester to the role of popular hero and tragic victim of Richard's machinations; in its deliberate garbling of historical fact; and in its early use of the humane elements of history.

The third play, which describes the tragic closing years of the unfortunate king, is the eloquent Richard II of Shakespeare, 1595–6.

Not to be outdone by the vogue of these chronicle plays, two contemporary poets, Samuel Daniel and Michael Drayton, immediately issued poetical versions of Richard's career. In 1595, Daniel published the *Civil Wars,* which covered in Books I–II the entire reign of Richard; and Drayton in his *England's Heroicall Epistles* (1597) introduced two poetical letters entitled *Queene Isabell to Richard the second,* and *Richard the second to Queen Isabell.*

The life of Richard II in these numerous forms bears, has been noted, an important relation to the political temper of the time. His deposition and murder had been merely the beginning of those fierce dissensions and conflicts between the houses of York and Lancaster that tore the breast of England and brought destruction to her kings; not until the accession of the Tudors had England and her royalty been able to enjoy comparative peace and security. Even then the strife between Protestant and Catholic under Queen Mary could hardly allay fears of future trouble; and on ascending the throne, Elizabeth with her councillors had all she could do to discover and suppress the intrigues of Mary Stuart and Philip II, supported by Catholic sympathizers, and directed by a scheming Pope. In fact the Queen had the spectre of civil uprising continually before her—a fear which sometimes became partially realized when Essex and his followers sowed dissension in her own court. Amid such threatening conditions any description of civil strife, or of deposed kings, whether appearing in literature,

or in the theatres, was extremely distasteful to her, fraught
as it was with peril lest it excite disgruntled factions to
rebellion.   And unfortunately for her, it was just these
tragedies of civil wars and falls of kings in the vivid
chronicles of Holinshed and Froissart that stimulated the
imagination of the Tudor playwrights; consequently when
Elizabeth was not confronted by rebellion in actuality, she
was forced to witness it continually vaunted on the stage
before her restless and excitable subjects.

. Perhaps, by 1590 Marlowe had portrayed in pitying terms
the downfall, deposition and murder of Edward II in a
drama that created the vogue of chronicle plays and offered
a model that succeeding playwrights were quick to employ.
Moreover, his success was followed by the huge tetralogy
of the Henry VI plays and Richard III, which were doubtless conceived and designed, though not completed by him.
About the same time another dramatist dared to go a step
farther in *Woodstock* and joining sympathies with the
people to glorify rebellion and to arouse admiration for a
popular hero in revolt against a weak but tyrannical king.
In *Woodstock*, as Professor Keller has noted, not only are
several passages apparently derived from Edward II, but
conceptions of character and situations as well.[3]   Both Edward and Richard are surrounded by contrasted groups of
favorites and seditious nobles—Queen Anne in *Woodstock*
is the counterpart of Queen Isabella in *Edward II;* in each
play Prince Richard and Prince Edward throw off the
irksome guardianship respectively of Gloucester and Mortimer; and both plays exhibit with tragic intensity the fall
of royal blood from high estate.   Moreover, Queen Elizabeth might well feel alarmed at *Woodstock*, which veritably
outdid *Edward II* by daring to glorify the rebellious and

[3] Shakespeare Jahrbuch, XXV, pp. 21–32.

intriguing uncle of Richard II, and thus to sanction and
encourage whether explicitly, or implicitly the spirit of
sedition. The fact that *Woodstock* was never printed seems
to demonstrate either that it received the condemnation of
the censor, or that the author did not dare to publish.

Finally Shakespeare turned his attention to the Richard
story and concluded it by eloquently portraying the deposition of the unhappy monarch. Although Shakespeare
perhaps did not make a conscious continuation of *Woodstock,* it seems clear that he presupposed familiarity with
the play on the part of his audience, and consequently
plunged immediately into the trial by combat between Herford and Mowbray, incited by Woodstock's foul murder,
fully assured that the spectators would pick up the thread
of history where his predecessor had dropped it. Perhaps,
on this account too, Shakespeare omitted the comic treatment which had been effective in *Woodstock,* and followed
with greater historical accuracy his Holinshed, in opposition to his predecessor who had mingled fact with fancy
and humor.[4]

Moreover, in emulation of Marlowe's *Edward II,* an indebtedness now well established, Shakespeare presented the
study of the same royal weakness under similar circumstances. Here also are the quarrels of contrasted groups
of nobles and favorites; the ensuing battles, the overthrow
and public deposition, incarceration and horrible death of
the royal protagonist. In the final scenes the parallel is
especially striking, when both monarchs abjectly remove
their crowns with similar doleful protests and moralizings.

Such pictures continually presented on the stage finally
brought condemnation from Queen Elizabeth. Though
Shakespeare's play was probably written in full form

[4] Notice may be made in this connection of Professor Keller's
parallel passages from Woodstock and Richard II.

during the years 1595–7, none of the quartos that appeared
in Elizabeth's lifetime dared to include the Parliament
scene and the deposing of Richard. And when Sir John
Hayward gave offense by publishing in 1599 a *History of
the First Part of the Life and Reign of Henry IV*, he was
imemdiately censured and thrown into prison by the Star
Chamber. In the trial of Essex in the February of the
following year, some of Essex's band hired Shakespeare's
company to give "the play of the deposyng and kyllyng of
Kyng Richard the second" to incite the people to rebellion.
At the trial Augustine Phillips, an actor in defense of the
company, held "the play of Kyng Rychard to be so old &
so long out of vse as that shold have small or no Company
at yt," but that for "xls more then their ordynary for yt"
they had consented to play it on the night of the Essex
Rebellion. This was, of course, Shakespeare's *Richard II.*
Syr Gelly Meyricke also stated that this drama presented
"Kyng Harry iiijth and the kyllyng of Kyng Rychard the
second played by the Lord Chamberlein's players, and at
the Globe."[5] *Camden's Annals* also records the statement
"quod exoletam tragoediam de tragica abdicatione Regis
Ricardi Secundi in publico theatro coram conjurationis
participibus data pecunia agit curasset." Finally, shortly
before Queen Elizabeth's death William Lambard, as
quoted by John Nichols,[6] thus describes the Queen reading
a volume of *Pandecta Rotulorum:* "So her Majestie fell
upon the reign of Richard II, saying, 'I am Richard II,
Know ye not that?' W.L. 'Such a wicked imagination
was determined and attempted by a most unkind Gent., the
most adorned creature[7] that ever your Majestie made.'
Her Majestie 'He that will forget God will also forget his

[5] Domestic State Papers, Elizabeth, cclxxxiii, 78 and 85.

[6] Progresses of Queen Elizabeth, III, 552.

[7] Essex.

benefactors; this *tragedy was played 40 times in the open streets and houses.'* "

Another non-extant play on the same invidious subject, entitled *perce of extone* (Henslowe's diary; Greg. I, 85), and written by Wilson, Dekker, Drayton and Chettle, very likely was the rival of Shakespeare's play among those forty performances of which Elizabeth complained.

The remaining chapters will explain how far the translation of Froissart by Lord Berners was ultimately responsible for this picture of Richard II in the plays and poems which caused so much disturbance. Special chapters have been given to each version and as in the discussion of Edward III, quotations from the chronicles have been appended under references to the work in question. With these sources before the reader, the parts derived from Froissart and those from other sources may be easily determined.

CHAPTER VI

THE LIFE AND DEATH OF JACK STRAW

The Life and Death of Jack Straw was entered on the Stationers' Register as an 'enterlude of lyf' on October 23, 1593. The first quarto bearing on the title page the date 1593, but in the printer's notice at the end, 1594, was issued with the title *The Life and Death of Jacke Straw a notabel Rebell in England; who was kild in Smithfield by the Lord Maior of London. Printed at London by John Danter, and are to be solde by William Burley at his shop in Gratious-Street over against Leaden Hall 1594.* The copyright was transferred with other plays to Thomas Pauyer in 1604, and the second quarto was issued for him in the same year. Although both quartos are badly mutilated, and bear signs of careless workmanship, the first is more accurate than the second. W. C. Hazlitt edited the second quarto for his edition of Dodsley, a reprint containing many textual errors in addition to those of the original. In 1901 H. Schütt reprinted the first quarto in his Kiel dissertation on *Jack Straw,* and with the aid of Holthausen, corrected the text and added a useful discussion. All references to the play here are based upon this edition.

The Life and Death of Jack Straw presents a vivid picture in four acts of the famous Peasants' Revolt of 1381, led by Wat Tyler and Jack Straw. The first three acts portray the uprising from its beginning to the death of Jack Straw, the protagonist, by the sword of Walworth, the Mayor of London. The last act describes the execu-

101

tion of Wat Tyler, and the mad priest, John Ball; and the knighting of the Lord Mayor.

In his introduction to the play, Schütt traces the sources of Jack Straw to the Chronicles of Holinshed, Grafton and Stow. Inasmuch as all of his selections from Holinshed are found in more complete form in either Stow or Grafton, it is difficult to understand why he quoted Holinshed at all. This error becomes more puzzling when it is realized that both Stow and Grafton contain sources that Holinshed does not afford: e. g., Holinshed lacks a necessary passage in John Ball's Sermon, and an account of the attack on the Flemings, both of which are in Stow; and Grafton provides the Sir John Morton episode of which Holinshed makes no mention. The review of Berners' influence on English chronicles in Chapter III, noted that Grafton took Berners' version of the Wat Tyler Rebellion verbatim, with the exception of a few additions from Fabian; but since one of Fabian's passages is reproduced in the text of the play, it is evident that Grafton was the chronicle consulted and that although the subject matter came originally from Froissart, Berners' translation of it was only indirectly the source of the play. (See sources for III, 1 and 2 ff.) Stow's share in these sources is merely supplementary. The following diagram conveniently illustrates the relations of the play to the sources and originals.

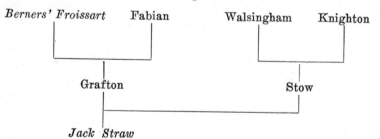

Although the following quotations from Grafton will often

obviously accord with the selections of Schütt, it has seemed best, while omitting the useless quotations from Holinshed, to give more complete extracts from Grafton in order to substantiate fully the large indebtedness of the author of *Jack Straw* to his chronicle. It should be noted at the outset, however, that the chronicles do not agree in the use of the names Wat Tyler and Jack Straw. Although these men are always two distinct leaders of the uprising, certain events ascribed to Jack Straw in one chronicle are given to Wat Tyler in another, and vice versa. Jack Straw is a nickname for John Tyler, probably a brother of Wat Tyler.[1]

SOURCES FOR JACK STRAW

ACT I

John Tyler slays the King's tax collector for insulting his daughter. Parson Ball instigates a rebellion among the commons.

SCENE ONE.

Grafton, I, 416. " And in this yere a Parliament was called, and therin was graunted to the king foure pence euery man and woman beyng of the age of xiiij yeres and upward, that were within the realme, at the which Subsidy the people did greatly murmure and much mischief came thereof, as in the yere followyng shall appere. But yet with that money and armie was prepared and sent ouer . . . passed the water of Some . . . and after lodged them betwene the newe Towne and Sens " (The last sentence is the source for Act I, scene 2, lines 1–9).

Stow, 294. " This tumult thus begun in Kent by meane of sir Simon Burley, was also increased by diuers other actions in other places amongst the which as I finde noted in a Chronicle sometimes belonging to the Monastery of St. Albans one of the collectors of the grotes, or pole Money, coming to the house of one

---

[1] For further discussion on this subject see Eng. Hist. Review, Vol. 21, p. 106.

John Tylar, in the towne of Dartford in Kent, demanded of the Tylar's wife, for her husbad, herselfe, her servaunts, & for their daughter (a young mayden) euery one of them a grote, which the Tylar's wife denied not to pay, sauing for her daughter who she said was but a child, not to be counted a woman: quoth the collector that will I soone wit, and taking the mayden, turned her up to search whether shee were undergrowne with haire or not, (for in many places they made the like triall) whereupon her mother cried out, neighbours came running in: and her husband being at worke in the same towne, tyling of an house, when he heard thereof, caught his lathing staffe in his hand, and ranne reaking home where reasoning with the Collector, who made him so bold the Collector answering with stout words & strake at the Tylar, whereupon the Tylar auoiding the blow, smote the Collector with his lathing staffe, that the braines flew out of his head, where through great noyse arose in the streetes and the poore people being glad, every one prepared to support the said John Tylar. Thus the Commons being drawne together, went to Maidstone, and from thence backe again to Blackeheath, and so in short time they stirred all the countrey. . . . These Commons had to their Chapeleine or Preacher a wicked Priest, called, Sir John Ball, who counsailed them to destroy all the Nobility, and Cleargy, so that there should be no Bishop in England, but one Archbishoppe, which should bee himself and that there should not bee aboue two religious persons in one house, and their possessions should be deuided among the layse men for the which doctrine they held him as a Prophet."

Parson Ball's Sermon (lines 45–78).

Stow, p. 294. "This man a twentie yeeres together and more preached in diuers places those things which he newe to be liking to the common people, slandering aswel ecclesiastical persons . . . he was committed to prison by Simon the Archbishop of Canterbury, & William Bishop of London, where hee prophecyed that hee should bee deliuered by twentie thousand of his friendes which came to passe in the foresaid time of troubles, when all prisons were broken up and the prisoners driven forth and when he was so deliuered, he followeth them, instigating them to commit much evill, and preaching that so it ought to be done. And that his doctrine might infect the more number of people, at Blackheath, where there were many thousands of the commons assembled, he began his Sermon in this manner.

When Adam dolue & Eue Span
Who was then a Gentleman?

And continuing his begunne Sermon, he sought by the word of the Proverbe which he towke for his Theame, to introduce, & proouue that from the beginning, all were made alike by nature, and that bondage or servitude was brought in by uniust oppression of naughty men, against the will of God; for if it hadde pleased God to haue made bondmen, hee woulde haue appointed them from the beginning of the world, who should haue bin slaue and who Lord. They ought to consider therefore, that nowe there was a time giuen them by God in the which, laying aside the yoke of continuall bondage, they might, if they woulde enjoy their long wished for libertie. . . . First, the Archbishop & great men of the kingdom were to be slaine: after, Lawyers, Justicars, & Questmongers: lastly whomsoeuer they knewe like hereafter to be hurtfull to the commons they should dispatch out of the land, for so might they purchase safety to themselues hereafter, if the great men beeing once taken away, there were among them equall libertie, all one nobilitie and like dignitie, and semblable authoritie or power. These, and many such madde devises he preached, which made the common people to esteeme of him in such manner, as they cryd out, he should be *Archybyshop of Canterbury & Chancellor of the Realme,* for hee onely deserued the honour. . . ." (Cf. lines 85, 86. This sentence is not in Holinshed.)

Wat Tyler is chosen leader of the rebels (lines 86–117).

Gr., I, 418. "And they made to themseulves certeine Capitaines, named Watte Tyler, Jacke Straw, and John Ball and other, of the whiche companye, Watte Tyler was the chiefe, and he was a Tyler in deede and an ungracious Patrone."

SCENE TWO.

Gr., I, 419. "This rebellion was well knowen in the kinges Court, before anye of these people began to Styrre out of any of their houses: But the king nor hys counsayle prouided not remedie therefore in due tyme (p. 421). Then their Capteynes Watte Tyler, Jacke Straw, Jack Shepard, and other, to the number of *XX Thousand,* went through London, and came to Sauoy. . . ." (Cf. line 55.)

SCENE THREE.

With this scene begins the episode of Sir John Morton, who was forced by the rebels to carry their complaint to King Richard. The story is not found in Stow or *Holinshed;* Grafton transcribed it from Berners' Froissart.

Gr., I, 419. "And when they were come *to Rochester* . . . they went to the *Castel* there, and tooke the Knight that had the rule thereof who was called Sir John Motton: and they sayde unto him. Sir John, you must go with us and ye shalbe our souereigne Capteyne, and doe that we will haue you doe. The Knight made many excuses very honestly and discretely but it auayled him nothing, for they sayde unto him, Sir John, if ye do not as we will haue you do, ye are but dead. . . . And whyle the lewde Company lay on *Blackheth,* they agreed the next day, which was Wednesday, to sende syr John Motton (whom they called their Knyght) to the king."

SCENE FOUR.

Scene four introduces the Queen Mother, and continues the John Morton episode.

Gr., I, 420. "But when they had well bethought themselues, they wylled Syr John Motton to say to the King that they desyred to speake with him, because that to none other they woulde open their griefes. The aforesayde Knight durst doe none other, but passed ouer the Thames and came to the Towre, praiyng to speake with the king. The king and they that were with him in the Towre, desirous to here newes, wylled that the knight should come unto them. And at that tyme there were present with the king, first the princesse his mother, and hys two brethren, the Erle of

Kent, and the Lord John Holland, the *Erle of Salisburie* . . . *the Archebishop of Cantorbury, the Lord of Saint Johns,*[2] Sir Robert of Namure . . . *the Maiour of London,* and dyuers other notabel citizens.

Thys knight syr John Motton, who was well knowen among them for he was one of the kinges officiers. He kneeled downe before the king, and sayde. My redouted Lorde, let it not displease your grace, the message that I must shew unto you, for deare syr, it is by force and agaynst my will, Sir John, sayde the king, saye what ye will, I holde you excused, Sir the commons of your realme hath sent me unto you, for to desyre you to come and speake with them on Blackheth, for they desyre to speake with you and none other. And syr ye neede not to haue any doubt of your person, for they will doe you no hurte, for they holde and will holde you fortheir king; But Sir, they say they will shew you diuers things the which shall be right necessary for you to take heede of, when they speake with you, of the which thinges I haue no charge to shewe you: But I humbly beseeche you, to geue me your aunswere, such as may appease them and that they maye knowe for truth that I haue spoken with you, for *they haue my children in hostage* untill I returne agayne unto them; and if I returne not agayne, they will sley my choldren incontynent. Then sayde the king, ye shall haue answere forthwith.

Then the king toke counsayle what was best for him to doe, and it was anone determined that the nexte morning the king would go downe by water, and without fayle speak with them, by the Thames side, whether he wylled that a certeine of them should come unto him."

The dramatist consulted the following passages for lines 1–52 and 137–157 which describe the fear of the Queen.

Gr., I, 419. " The same day that these unhappie people of Kent were commyng to London, there returned from Canterbury the kinges mother Princess of Wales. . . . She was in great jeopardy to haue beene lost . . . howbeit God kept her. . . . And the same tyme *Richard her sonne,* was at the Tower of London,

[2] The Lord Treasurer.

and *there his mother found him* and with him there was *the Erle of Salisbury*, the *Archebishop of Cauntorbury.*

ACT II

SCENE ONE.

In this comic scene Nobs (a survival of the old Vice of the Morality and Interlude) steals a goose from Tom Miller. The sentence "It is good to make prouision for peradventure we shall lacke virtuals" is reminiscent of Grafton (I, p. 420) "And the fourth part of them fasted for lack of virtuall, which greued them muche."

SCENE TWO.

King Richard frightened by clamors of the mob avoids the appointed meeting by the Thames, and turns his barge toward London.

Gr., I, 420–1. "In the morning being Thursday, the king being accompanied wyth the Erle of Salsburie . . . tooke his barge and rowed downe along the Thames to Detforde, and there were come doune and the hill aboue ten thousand of the afore-sayd persons, to see and speake with the king.

And when they sawe the kings Barge coming, they began to showte, and made such a crie as if all the Deuills in hell had bene among them. And they had brought with them Sir John Motton, to the entent that if the king had not come, they would haue hewen hym all to pieces, and so they promysed hym.

And when the king and his Lords sawe the demeanour of the people, the stowtest hearted of them that were with the king were afrayed. And the Lordes counsayled the king not to take any landyng there, but to towe up and doune the ryuer. . . . Then the king was counsayled to return agayne to the Towre of London, and so he did. And when they sawe that, they were enflamed with wrath. . . . Then they cryed all wyth one voyce, *let us go to London,* and so they tooke their waye thether, and in their goyng they bet downe the *Lawyers houses* without all mercie, and many other houses of such as had officies under the king."

Scene Three.

Scene three introduces two new characters,—Sir John
Newton and Spencer, a bargeman,—whom the dramatist
took from Stow.   Pages 288–9 of Stow's chronicle contain
an episode (unconnected with the play) between Wat Tyler
and a Sir John Newton.   The name Spencer is taken at
random from a Sir Henry Spencer mentioned on page 291.
These characters discuss the flight of the king to London.

Scene Four.

The mob pillages London and its suburbs.

Gr., I, 421.   " And specially they brake up the kinges prisons,
as the *Marshalsey, and the kinges Benche,* and delyuered freely
all the prisoners that were within.   And at the bridge foote,
because the Gates were closed, they threatened sore the Citizens
of London, sayeng how they would brenne all the suburbes and
also sley all the commons of the Citie, and set the Citie on fyre.
And within the Citie were a great number of their affinitie, and
they sayde: why doe not we let these good felowes, into the Citie?
they are oure felowes, and that that they doe is for us."

Scene Five.

St., 228.   ". . . . they fetched . . . Flemings . . . in other places
of the Cittie, and in *Southwarke,* all which they beheaded, except
they could plainly pronounce *bread and cheese,* for if their speech
sounded any thing on *brot,* or *cawse,* off went their heads, as a
sure marke they were Flemings."

Conference between King and mob.

Gr., I, 423.   " And the king entered in among them, and spake
unto them gently and sayde.   A good people, I am your king,
what lacke ye? what doe ye saye?   Then such as heard him sayd,
that ye will make us free for euer, our selues, our heyres, and oure
landes, and that we be called no more bondmen, nor from hence-
forth so to be reputed or taken.   Sirs, sayde the king, I doe
gladly graunt your request; withdrawe you home to your owne
houses, and into suche Villages as ye came from, and leaue behind

you of euery Village two or three, and I wyll *cause wrytinges to be made and seale them with my seale,* the which they shall haue with them, conteining euery thing that ye demaund. . . . These wordes quieted well the common people. . . . And the king sayde also one worde, the which greatly contented them, and that was: syrs, among you good men of Kent, ye shall haue one of my banners, and ye of *Essex* another. . . . And also I *pardon euery thing that ye haue done hetherto,* so that ye folowe my Banners, and returne home to your houses. They all aunswered they would so doe. Thus these *people departed and went to* London. . . .

But yet great venome remayned behind, for Watte Tyler, Jacke Strawe and other of their Captaines sayde, they would not so depart, and there agreed unto them mo then **XXX** thousand: And thus they abode stil, and made no haste, neyther to haue the kings wryting or Seale, for their ententes was to haue spoyled the Citie. . . . When it drewe toward nyght, the king came to the Towre in the Royall, where the Princesse his mother beyng in great feare had remayned all that day, to comfort her and taried there with her all that night."

Gr., I, 424–5. (Cf. lines 75 to end of Sc. 2.) "On Saturday, the next day in the forenoone, the king had bene at Westminster, and came from thence on the backsyde through Holborne into London, and thought to haue ridden to the Tower, and as he came ouer Smithfielde, he sawe there Watte Tyler, Jacke Strawe, and their companie assembled together, which caused him a little to stay, and considering them wel, they seemed to be nere unto the number of **XX** thousand. . . . And when Watte Tyler[3] sawe the king, he sayd to his company, yonder is the king, I will go speake with him, stirre not you, quoth he to the people, from hence, except I make you a signe, and when I make you a signe, come on together, and slay them all (except the king) But do the king no hurt, for he is yong, and we shall rule him as we list, and lead him with us round about England, and so without doubt we may be Lordes of the realme. And therewith he spurred his horse, and came to the king, so nere him that hys horse touched the kinges horses heade as they roade, and the first worde that he

[3] Jack Straw in the play.

sayde unto the king was this, Sir King seest thou all yonder people? ye truely sayd the king, wherefore askest thou that? Because sayde he, they be all at me commandement, and haue sworne to me fayth and trouth, to do all that I will haue them. In a good tyme sayde the king, be it so. . . . With those wordes Watte Tyler cast his euen on a Squier that was ther with the king, and bare the kinges sworde. And Watte Tyler hated greatly the same Squier, for wordes that had passed the day before betwene them, and sayde unto him, what, sayest he, art thou there? *Geue me thy dagger.* Nay sayd the Squier, that I will not do, wherefore should I geue it thee? The king beheld the squier and sayd, *geue it him.* And when Watte Tyler had it, he began to play wyth it in his hand, turning of it: And then he sayd againe to the Squier *geue me that sworde,* nay sayd he, *it is the kings* sworde, thou art not worthie to haue it for thou art but a knaue. *And there were no mo here but thou and I, thou durst not demaund any such things of me,* neyther to speake as thou hast spoken, *for as much Golde as would lye in yonder Abbey:* By my fayth sayd Watte Tyler, *I will neuer eate meate untill I haue thy head.*

And with those wordes the Maior of London came to the King, with Xij horses well armed under their coates, and so he brake the prease, and saw and heard the demeanor of Watte Tyler in the presence of the King, and he sayde unto him, Ha thou knaue, howe *darest thou be so bolde in the kinges presence* to speake suche words, it is to much to suffer thee so to do. Then the king began to chafe, and sayde to the Maior, set handes on him. And when the king had sayd so, Watte Tyler sayde to the Maior, a Gods name, what haue I sayde to displease thee? Yes truely quoth the Maior, thou false stinking knaue, shalt thou speake thus in the presence of the king my naturall Lorde? I wish neuer to liue, except thou dearely by it. And with those wordes the Maior drewe out his sworde, and stroke Watte Tyler, such a stroke on the head that he fell downe at the feete of his horse. . . . Then the unhappy people there assembled, perceyuyng their Capteyne slaine began to murmure among themselves and sayd: A, *our Capteine is slaine,* let us go slay them all. . . . The king departed from all his company. . . . And when he came to his ungracious people . . . sayd unto them, Sirs what ayleth you, you shall haue no Capteine but me, *I am and will be your king and Capteine.* . . ."

ACT III

SCENES ONE AND TWO.

After pillaging London, burning records, slaying nobles, and frightening the Queen Mother, the rebels demand a conference with the king, who gives them partial satisfaction. Another conference follows at which the Mayor of London slays Jack Straw.

Two facts at this point prove that Grafton's Chronicle was the source of the play and not Berners' Froissart.

1. Berners' Froissart does not mention the destruction of the records and the books of law.

2. Grafton supplies these details in an interpolated sentence which he took from Fabian, as designated in the following passage:

Gr., I, 421. " Then their Capteynes Watte Tyler, Jacke Straw, Jack Shepard, and other, to the number of XX thousand, went through London, and came to *Sauoy*, which then was a goodly place, and perteyned to the Duke of Lancaster. And when they were entered therein, they first slue the keepers thereof and then spoyled and robbed the house. And when they had so done, they set fyre on it, and cleane consumed and destroyed it: and then came unto the temple and other innes of court, and spoyled the *bookes* of law and the *recordes* of the counter, and set all the *prisoners of newegate* and the counters at large.[4] And when they had this done, then they went streight to the goodly Hospitall of the Rhodes, called *Saint Johns* beyond *Smithfielde*,

---

[4] Cf. Fabian, p. 530. ''Tha they entryd the cytie & serchid the *Temple and other innes of court, & spoylyd* theyr placys & brent theyr bokys of lawe, . . . & toke with them all seyntwary men, & the *prysons of Newgate*, & . . . of bothe *Counters*, & distroyed theyr registers & *bokis*.''

and spoyled that likewyse, and then consumed it with fyre."
(*The italicized words appear in speeches of Tom Miller and Nobs*
in Scene two and in the Lord Mayor's speech in Scene one.)

Attack on the Queen Mother.

Gr., I, 422. " Also these wretches entred into the Princesse
Chamber, and brake her head, with the which she was so sore
afrayde, that she sowned, and so was taken . . . to a place called
the Royall and there she was all that day and night, as a woman
halfe deade, untill shee was comforted with the king her sonne, as
ye shall after here."

Act IV

Act IV portrays the punishment of Wat Tyler and Parson Ball and the king's pardon of the other rebels. The
play ends with the knighting of Walworth, Lord Mayor of
London.

Gr., I, 427. " But nowe sayeth *Froyssart,* John Ball, and Jack
Strawe[5] were found hidden in an olde house, where they had
thought to haue stollen awaue, but they could not, for they were
accused by their awne company. Of the taking of them, the
king and his Lordes were glad, he caused their heades to be
striken of, and Watte Tylers also, and commaunded them to be
set upon London bridge . . . (428) and the rest he pardoned, and
so all the realme was quieted." (426.) There the king made foure
knightes. The one the Maiour of London, Syr Nycholas Walworth, Sir John Standishe and Syr Nycholas Brembre."

A comparison of the passages given above with the text
of the drama shows that Grafton's Chronicle was the source
of the whole play with the exception of two scenes (I, 1;
II, 5) and two names of characters. It has also been noted
that Grafton's account of the rebellion is largely copied
from Berners' Froissart, but that the interpolation from

5 Wat Tyler in the play.

Fabian proves that Grafton, and not Froissart was the direct source of the play. Many words and phrases taken directly from Grafton's text leads one to believe that the dramatist wrote the play with the chronicle open before him. It might possibly be contended that Grafton supplied the material for the two scenes ascribed here to Stow, since the former also has an account of John Ball's sermon, and a description of the Flemish slaughter. It is unfair to make the contention, however, since the passages from Stow resemble in wording the lines of these scenes as closely as the passages of Grafton resemble the lines in the rest of the play. Following the custom of other chronicle playwrights, the author of *Jack Straw* supplemented Grafton, his main source, with a few details from Stow, his minor source.

CHAPTER VII

A TRAGEDY OF KING RICHARD II (WOODSTOCK)

The anonymous *Tragedy of King Richard, concluding the Murder of the Duke of Gloucester at Calais* was inaccessible to students of the drama until 1870, when J. O. Halliwell printed copies of the play in quarto from the Egerton manuscript in the British Museum. The text of this edition, however, was proved unreliable by Professor Wolfgang Keller, who in the Shakespeare Jahrbuch, 1899, volume XXXV, published the first accurate text with helpful notes and discussions of sources. He also assigned as a reasonable date for *Woodstock* (or 1 R 2, as he names the play) 1591–2, or between Marlowe's *Edward II* and Shakespeare's *Richard II.*

The drama, as has been noted, covers the historic period 1382–1397, from the marriage of Richard and Anne of Bohemia, to the murder of Woodstock, Duke of Gloucester. Yet it is difficult to understand why Halliwell entitled the play *A Tragedy of King Richard,* because Woodstock, and not Richard, is the protagonist and victim. A search for the historical sources of the hero's career presents a problem very different from that of *Edward III* or *Jack Straw,* and one far more baffling and difficult. To observe the close adaptations of the chronicle by the dramatist in the preceding plays requires but little comparative study. For *Woodstock,* however, no one chronicle suffices. The author unquestionably had several chronicles at his disposal and selected details from them haphazard, without the slightest regard for chronology or historical accuracy. He increased

115

the confusion further by frequently interrupting the main action with comic scenes of his own invention.

Professor Keller diligently gathered from Holinshed and Stow all passages from these chronicles which have a possible bearing upon the play. A comparison of the text with his quotations, however, leaves much to be desired, for whole scenes and details of important scenes remain without sources. But an examination, restricted to any one chronicle, leads to the same inadequate result. Any one of the three chronicles of Berners, Grafton or Holinshed, could furnish the main outline of history as found in the play.[1] But, as Keller says, two or three passages from Stow must be cited for details that no other chronicle mentions, although Stow's main narrative is inadequate in nearly all other respects. Grafton's chronicle, which critics have heedlessly neglected, affords on the whole a source more consistent, because more detailed than Holinshed's; while an examination of Berners' translation reveals sources for events, characters and details which are not found in other chronicles. While the accounts in all the English chronicles concerning the troubles between Gloucester and Richard are briefly rehearsed in three or four pages, Froissart's narrative of twenty-nine pages is paticularly detailed,—a fact easily accounted for, since Froissart was in England during the quarrel. Furthermore he was personally acquainted with R. Surrey,[2] probably the Surrey of the play, and mourned the execution of Burleigh,[2] one of Richard's favorites. Froissart's chronicles combined either with Grafton, or with Holinshed provide a satisfactory source

[1] Fabian's account is too cursory to be given any consideration. Grafton abandoned Berners, and employed different accounts from English sources. Holinshed made use of Thomas Walsingham. Stow practically neglected the events.

[2] Froissart, pp. 615, 281.

for the whole play, plus the necessary additions from Stow. As there is slight preference between Grafton and Holinshed, references from both have been given, the one quoted being the more satisfactory account. Where Berners' account coincides with others, it has been given the preference only when it is more in accord with the details of the play. Thus, when a single authority is quoted, that is the *only* source; when more than one authority is cited, the quotation is from the chronicle that resembles most closely the text of the play.

ACT I

SCENE ONE.
  Richard's plot to kill his uncles.

Holinshed, II, 774.[3] (Also in Grafton, Stow and Fabian). (for lines 1–105.) "Hereupon (as was said, whether trulie or otherwise, the lord knoweth) by a conspiracie begun twixt the king and such as were most in favor with him, it was deuised, that the duke of Gloucester (as principall) and such other lords as fouored the knights and burgesses in their sute, against the earle of Suffolke, and were otherwise against the king in his demand of monie, should be willed to a supper in London, there to be murthered. But the duke comming by some meanes to understand of this wicked practise, had no desire to take part of that supper, where such sharpe sauce was prouided."

Admiral Arondell, his sea victory and booty. Referred to in Sc. 1, 78–92; Sc. 3, 140–148; 175–182; 223–229.

Ber., II, pp. 374–376. (Holinshed, Grafton and Stow.) "as for corn whyne salte bacone, and other provision, they foude ynoughe, for there was more than four hundred tonne of wyne in the towne . . . and caryd with them moche wine . . . and so entred into their vesselles. . . ."

---

[3] The references to Holinshed whenever cited in this chapter repeat Keller's selections, S.J. XXXV.

Woodstock discreetly persuades Lancaster, Surrey, Arondell and York not to plot against Richard.

Ber., II, 275–6. (Grafton.) (W. 111–215.) "Than the duke answered and sayde, fayre sirs, I haue herde you well speke, but I alone can nat remedy this mater; howbeit I se well ye haue cause to coplayne and so hathe all other people; but though I be uncle to the kynge and sonne to a kyng, though I shulde speke therof, yet nothyng shal be done for all that, for the kyng my nephue hath suche cousayle as rowe about hym, whome he beleueth better than hymselfe, whiche cousayle ledeth hym as they lyste. . . ."

The following figure would seem to be borrowed directly from Berners unless the resemblance be a mere coincidence.

WOODSTOCK, lines 141–2	BERNERS, II, 281
" *Wood.*	Ye haue herde often tymes
Enough, enough	sayde, that if the heed be sicke,
Good brother; I haue found	all the membres can nat be
out the disease:	well; the malady must first be
When the head akes, the body	pourged."
is not healthfull."	

SCENE TWO.

Tressilian made Lord Chief Justice of England.   Gr. I, 434; St. 292; Hol. II, 784; Berners, II, 278.

SCENE THREE.

Marriage of Richard and Anne of Bohemia (W. 1–150).

Ber., I, 668–9. (Grafton, Holinshed, Stow, Fabian.) There is little choice of accounts here. Froissart and Grafton have more elaborate accounts of the wedding than the others.

Queen Anne introduces side-saddles.   This detail is found only in *Stow*, 295. (W. 57–62.)

"Also noble women. . . rode on side saddles, after the example of the Queene who first brought that fashion into this land, for before women were used to ride astride like men."

Plain speaking and stubbornness are traits of Gloucester's character.

Ber., II, 634–687, 277. (W. 14–24; 113–231.)
"Than sir Thomas Duke of Gloucester sayde, Sir, in the request and prayer of these good people, the commons of your realme, I se nothynge therin but ryght and reasone." (P. 277.)
(P. 684.) "Thus the duke of Gloucestre . . . whan the kyng dyd sende for him he wolde come at his pleasure, and sometyme nat a whyt; and whan he came to the kynge, he wolde be the laste shulde come an the first that wolde departe, and in counsayle what he had ones sayd of his opynion, he wolde haue it taken and accepted, else he wolde be displeased. . . ."

Richard confers official appointments upon his favorites.

Ber., II, 281. (W. 183–190.) "I saye it, because this duke of Irelande was so great with the kyng, that he ruled hym as he lyste. He and sir symon Burle[5] were two of the princypall cousaylours that the kynge had, for they hadde a long season gouerned the kynge and the realme; and they were had in suspects that they hadde gadered richesse without nombre. . . ."

Lancaster delegated to pacify the discontented people.

Ber., II, 686 (230–269). "These wordes or such lyke spoken by the duke of Lancastre apeased greatly the people who were sette to do yuell, by the settynge on of other."

Act II
Scene One.
The favorites urge Richard to kill Woodstock.
Ber., II, 690–1. (Hol.) "The kyng had as than but yonge

[4] Ireland is Tressilian in the play.
[5] Burle is Bushey in the play.

counsayle about hym, and they greatly douted the duke of Gloucestre, and oftentymes wolde saye to the kynge: Ryht dere sir,
it is a perylous thyng to serue you, for we haue sene suche as haue
serued you in tymes paste, and such as were ryght synguler in
your foure . . . yet your uncle the duke of Gloucestour caused
hym to dye shamefully . . . and, sir, we that sarue you nowe,
looke for the same rewarde: for whan your uncle cometh to you,
the whiche is nat often, we dare nat lyfte up our eyen to loke
upon any persone, *he loket so hye ouer us;* he thynketh we do
hym moche wrog that we be so nere about you as we be: wherfore,
sir, knowe for trouthe yt as long as he liueth there shall be no
peace in Englande. . . . Sir, ye be a kyng lost if ye take nat
goode hede to yourself. . . ."

The uncles appoint a Parliament at Westminster without
consulting Richard.

Ber., II, 285. "At last he understode that the kynges uncles,
and the newe counsayle of England, would kepe a secrete Parlya-
ment at Westminster. . . ."

Ber., II, 294. "Whan he came before hym, he humyled hymselfe greatlye to the kynge, and there shewed the kyng . . . that
if it were his pleasure to come to London to his palys of Westmynster, his uncles and mooste parte of the realme wolde be ryght
joyeous, elles they wyll be ryght sorie and yuell displeased. . . .
The yonge kynge . . . finally . . . refrayned his displeasure, by
the good meanes of the quene . . . and of some other wise
knightes that were about hym. . . ."

SCENE TWO.

Parliament at Westminster. King Richard proclaims his
right to the throne and dismisses his uncles.

Ber., II, 295. "The Archebysshoppe of Cauntorbury shewed
to the kynges uncles and counsayle that when Kynge Rycharde
was crowned Kynge of Englande and that euery man was sworne
and made theyr releues to hym . . . and a kynge out nat to
gouerne a royalme tyll he be XXI yeres of age. . . . The bysshop
sayd this because the kynge as then was but newlye come to the

age of XXI yeres. . . . And Kynge Richarde was in his chapell in his palys richly apareyled, with his *crowne on his heed*. . . ."

389. " Ye haue herde here before howe Kynge Richarde of Englande had some trouble: he agaynst his uncles, and his uncles agaynst hym, with other dyuers incydentes, as by the Duke of Ire-lande and other . . . and the archebysshop of Yorke was at a poynte to haue loste his benefyce and by the new counsaylers about the kyng, the lore Neuell . . . was as than put out of wages. . . ." *Page 690.* " These dukes sawe well that the busyness of Eng-lande began to be yuell, and parceyued that gret hatered en-creased dayly . . . they departed fro the kynges court . . . and went to their owne."

Holinshed, II, 798 ff. adds: " The earle of Arundell likewise unto whome the gouernment of the parlement was committed, and the admeraltie of the sea, was remooued."

Ber., II, 688. (Gr., I, 464: Hol. II, 838.) "for he thought hymselfe natte well assured amonge his uncles: for he sawe well howe they absented theymselfe fro his courte, and kept them at home at their owne houses, so that he was halfe in doute of them, and specially of the duke of Gloucestre, and so kepte dayly about hym a garde of a thousande archers."

Scene Three.

Consolation scene of the Queen, Duchess of Ireland and Duchess of Gloucester. Berners provides the source for the Duchess of Ireland's complaint (lines 10–12.)

Ber., II, 283. " The duke of Ireland . . . was in suche loue with one of the quene's damoselles . . . that he wolde gladly be duorsed fro his owne wife."

Act III

Scene One.

The Duchess of Gloucester appears only in Froissart.

The king devises blank charters for extorting more money from his realm.

Grafton, I, 471. " Also at thys tyme the king caused many

blacke chartres to be made, and forced men to signe and seal the
same, by the which he might whe he would undo any of his subjects.   But some write that it was for that he purposed to delyuer
Calice, and all his landes beyonde the Sea, to the French king,
and to shewe that al his subjectes had assented thereunto."   The
last sentence provides a source for Act IV, scene 1, lines 109–
113.   Holinshed II, page 848 ff. mentions the blank charters.

Richard's festival at Westminster.   (Lines 81–108.)

Stow, 319.   " This yeere (1398–99) the K. kept a most royall
Christmas, with euery day justings and running at the tile,
whereunto resorted such a number of people, that there was
euery day spent XXVIII or XXVI oxen, and three hundred
sheepe, besides foule without number.   Also the king caused a
garment for himselfe to be made of gold, siluer and precious
stones, to the value of 3000 markes."

Stow, 295.   (W. 52–58.)   " In this Queenes dayes, began the
destable use of piked shooes, tyed to their knees with chaines of
siluer and guilt."

SCENE TWO.

Woodstock, Lancaster and York at Plashy.

Ber., II, 684, 687.   " The duke of Gloucestre . . . wolde . . .
take his leaue and depart to his maner in Essex, called Plasshey
. . . (681)   At that tyme the Dukes of Lancastre nor of Yorke
were nat with the kynge for they began somewhat to dissymule,
for they sawe well that the people in Englande beganne to murmure in dyuers places on the state and rewle that the kynge kept,
and that the maters were lykely to go yuell . . . and all this came
by reasons of the duke of Gloucestre and his company.

The remainder of Act III is given over to comedy of the
dramatist's invention.

ACT IV

SCENE ONE.

Richard 'farms out the realm' to his favorites.

Grafton, I, 471.   (Hol.)   " The saiyng also was, that before his goyng into Ireland, he had let the realme to ferme to *Sir William Scrope*, Erle of Wiltshire, and then Treasurer of England, to *Sir John Bushe, Sir John Bagot* and *syr Henry Grene, knightes*, for the terms of xiiij yeres: By reason whereof they procured many men to be accused, and such as were accused, there was no remedye to diluer him, or them, but were he poore or riche, he must compounde and make his fine with those Tyrannes, at their will and pleasure."

SCENE ONE ⎫
SCENE TWO ⎬ (62–250.)

Gloucester's capture by Richard and his favorites.

Ber., II, 692. (Hol. II.) " King Richarde of England noted well these sayd wordes, ye which was shewed hym in secretuess, and lyke an ymaginatyfe price as he was, within a season after that his vncles of Lacastre and of Yorke were departed out of the courte, than the kynge toke more hardynesse on hym, and said to hymselfe: That fyrste it were better for hym that he shulde do hym no displeasure after: and bycause he could nat bring about his purpose alone, he dyscouered his mynde to such as he trusted best, as to therle marshall his cosyn erle of Nottyngham, and shewed hym his full mynde what he wolde do and haue to be doone. The erle marshall (who loued the kyng better than the duke of Glocestre dyde) kept the kynges purpose secrete, sauig to suche as he wolde be ayded by, for he coude nat do ye kynges pleasure alone. On a day the kyng in maner as goyng a hutynge, he rode to Haueryng Boure. a XX myle fro London in Essexe. and within XX myle of Plasshey, where the duke of Gloucestre helde his house: after dyner the kyng departed fro haueryng with a small copany, and cae to Plasshey about V. a clocke; ye weder was fayre and hote; so the kyng cae sodainly thyder about the tyme that the duke of Gloucestre had supped, for he was but a small eater, nor satte neuer long at dyner nor at supper. Wha he herde of the kynges comynge, he went to mete with hym in the myddes of the court, and so dyde the duchesse and her chyldren, and they welcomed the kynge, and the kyng entred into the hall, and so into a chambre: tha a borde was spredde for the kynges supper: the kynge satte nat long, and sayd at his fyrst commyng: Fayre vncle, cause fyue or sixe horses of yours to be sadylled, for I wyll praye you to ryde with me to London: for to morrowe the londoners wyll be before vs, and there wyll be also myne vncles of Lacastre and Yorke, with dyuers other noble men: for upon the londoners requestes I wyll be ordred accordyng to your counsayle; and comaunde your stewards to folowe you with your trayne to lodon, where they shall fynde you. The duke, who thought none yuell, lightly agreed to ye kynge; and whan the kyng had supped and rysen, euery thynge was redy: the kynge than toke a leaue of the duchesse and of her children, and lepte a horsebacke and ye duke with hym, accompanyed all onely but with seuyn seruanntes, thre squyers and foure yeomen, and tooke the waye of Bondelay, to take the playne waye, and to eschewe Bridwode and London comon hyghe waye: so they rode a great pace, and talked by the way with his vncle and he with hym, and so aproched to Stratforde on the ryuer of Thamise. Whan the kyng came nere to the busshment that he had layde, than he rode fro his vncle a great pace, and lefte hym somewhat behynde hym; than sodynly the erle Marshall with his bands came galopyng after the duke, and ouertoke hym and saide: Sir, I arest you in the kynges name. The duke was abasshed with that worde, and sawe well he was betrayed, and began to call loude after ye kyng: I can nat tell wheder the kyng herde hym or nat, but he turned nat, but rode forthe faster than he dyde before."

SCENE THREE.

Hol., II, 823. (Ber., Gr.) "This yeare on Whitsundaie being the seauenth of June, queene Anne departed this life, to the great greefe of hir husband king Richard, who loued hir intirelie. She deceassed at Shene, and was buried at Westminster. . . . The king tooke such a conceit with the house of Shene, where she departed this life, *that he caused the buildings to be throwne downe and defaced,* whereas the former kings of this land, being wearie of the citie, vsed customablie thither to resort, as to a place of pleasure, and seruing highlie to their recreation."

ACT V

SCENE ONE.

Murder of Gloucester. Berners is the only chronicle that describes in great detail,—three folio pages,—the capture and murder of Gloucester, though such scenes had been presented on the stage before in Marlowe's Edward II with which the author of Woodstock was certainly familiar. Holinshed makes a brief reference to Gloucester's death which he gathered from an "old French pamphlet." (II, 837.) Grafton's account of the capture is quite different, and owes nothing to Berners. The last prayer of Gloucester before his murder is found only in *Berners*, II, 692, 705–6.

"Ye haue herde here before of the couert hates that was bytwene kynge Rycharde of Englande, and his vncle Thomas duke of Gloucestre, whiche the kynge wolde bear no longar, but sayd, and also was counsayled, rather to distroye another man than hymselfe: and ye haue herde howe the kyng was at Plasshey, and by crafte and coloure, brought hym out of his owne house to London, and by the waye about X. or a XI. of the clocke in the nyght, therle marshall arested hym in the kynges name: and for all that he cryed after the kynge, yet the kynge made a deafe eare, and rode on before, and so the same nyght the kynge laye at the tower of London, but the duke of Gloucestre was otherwise lodged, for by force he was put into a barge, and out of the barge into a shyppe that laye in the Thamise, and the erle marshall with hym and all his company, and dyde so moche, that the nexte day by night they came to Calais, without knoledge of any man, excepte the kynges offycers of the sayd towne. . . ."

Page 706. "Whan the duke of Glocestre was brought to the castell of Calys, than he feared hymselfe greatlye, and said to the erle marshall: For what cause am I brought out of Englande hyder to Calais? Mythynke ye holde me as a prisoner: lette me go abrode and se the fortresse aboute. Sir, quod the marshall, that ye desyre I dare nat do it, for I haue the charge ypon you on

payne of my lyfe: the kynge my souerayne lorde is a lytell mys-
content with you, wherfore ye must take pacyence here for a
seasone, tyll I here other newes, and that shal be shortely by
goddes grace; for sir, as helpe me God, I am right sorie for your
trouble if I myght remedy it; but sir, ye knowe well I am sworne
to the kynge, wherfore I must obey, and so well I do, for sauynge
of myne honoure. The duke coude haue none other aunswere, but
by that he sawe he feared greatly his lyfe: and on a daye he
desyred a preest and sange masse before hym, that he myght be
confessed, and so he was a good leysar before the sacrament with
deuout herte, and *cryed God mercy and was sore repentant of all
his synnes; and in dede it was tyme so for hym so to do,* for his
dethe was nerer to hym than he was were of; for as I was en-
fourmed, whan he hadde dyned and was aboute to haue wasshen
his handes, there came into the chambre foure men and caste
sodaynlye a towell aboute the duke's necke, two at the one ende
and two at the other, and drewe so sore that he fell to the erthe,
and so they strangled hym and closed his eyen: and whan he was
deed they dispoyled him, and bare hym to his beed, and layde
hym bytwene the shetes all naked and his heed on a softe pyllowe,
and couered with clothes furred: and than they yssued out of the
chambre into the hall, well determyned what they wolde saye, and
sayde openly, howe a palueysye hadde taken the duke of Gloucestre the same night sodaynly, and so dyed."

SCENE TWO.

Lancaster and York take arms against Richard for mur-
dering Gloucester.

Ber., II, 707. (Gr.; Hol.) " What the dethe of ye duke of
Gloucestre was knowe by the dukes of Lancastre and of Yorke,
incotinent they knewe well that the kynge their nephue had
caused hym to be slayne and murdered at Calays. As than these
two dukes were nat toguyder, eche of the were at their owne
places; they wrote eche to other to knowe what were best to do,
and so they came to London, for they knewe well that the Londoners were nat content with the dethe of the duke their brother.
Whan they mette there toguyder, they tooke cousayle, and sayd:

Such dedes ought nat to be suffred, as to putte to dethe so hyghe a price, as was their brother for yuell wordes and false reportes; for they sayd, though he spake oftentymes of the breakyng of ye peace yet he neuer brake it, and bytwene sayenge and doyng is great difference, for by reason of wordes he ought nat to deserue dethe by such cruell punycion: these two dukes were in the case to haue put all Englande to great trouble, and there were ynowe redy to counsayle thereto, and specially them of the erle of Arundelles lynage, and of the erle of Staffordes, whiche was a great kynred in Englande."

Mourning of the Duchess of Gloucester and her appeal to Lancaster and York for aid (lines 45–61).

Ber., II, 705. "Ye maye well knowe whane the takynge of the duke was knowen at Plasshey, by the duchesse and her chyldren, they were sore troubled and abasshed, and thought well that the matter went nat well: the duchesse demaunded cousaile (what was best to do), of sir Johan Laquyham. The knight answered, that it was best to sende to his bretherne, the dukes of Lancastre and of Yorke, that they myght fynde some meanes to apeace the kinges dyspleasure, for he sayde he thought that the kyng wolde nat displease them. The duchesse dyd as the knyght counsayled her, and she sente incontynent messangers to these two dukes, who were farre asondre, who whanne they herde thereof were sore displeased, and sente worde agayne to the duchesse that she shuld be of good coforte, for they sayd they knew well the kyng wolde nat entreat hym but by laufull iudgement, for otherwise they coude nat suffre it; but as thanne they knewe natte where he was. The duchesse and her chyldren was somewhat conforted with their answere."

Scene Three.
Flight of Baggot.

Hol., II, 852 ff. (Gr.) "The lord treasurer Bushie, Bagot, and Greene, perceiving that the common would cleauve vnto, and take part with the duke, slipped awaie. . . . Bagot got him to

Chester, and so escaped into Ireland; the other fled to the castle of Bristow, in hope there to be in safetie."

Tresilian betrayed by his servant.

Ber., II, 285–287. (Gr. I, 456; Hol., taken from Grafton, Stow, 303.) "Therewith this sir Robert *Tryuillyen* . . . disguysed in maner of a poore marchaunt . . . came to London . . . and lerned what he colde. . . . He came and lodged at Westmynster. at last on a day a squyer of the duke of Gloucesters knewe hym, for he had often tymes ben in his company; . . .: Therwith the squyer entredde into the house where *Tryuylien* was . . . and toke hym, and so brought hym to the palays . . . (p. 287). sir Robert *Triuylien* was deyuered to the hangman and so ledde out of Westmynster, and there beheeded, and after haged on a gibet. Thus ended sir Robert *Triuylien*."

These quotations and references from various sources when compared with the text of the play will reveal how extensively the dramatist garbled his history. To mention the principal anachronisms,—the author made Tresilian chief justice at a time when the Duke of Ireland was Richard's most influential favorite. He ascribed the death of Tresilian who was killed by Woodstock, to Lancaster after Woodstock's death; he turned the squire, who took Tresilian prisoner, into Nobs, a Vice. He thrust the favorites of Richard's closing year Bushy, Bagot, and Greene into the places that Ireland, Burley, and others were then occupying. He had Richard dismiss Arundel as well as his uncles at the Westminster Parliament, but did not picture Richard as immediately ordering his execution. He postponed the death of Queen Anne, until just before the murder of Woodstock, when Richard was married to Queen Isabella. It is impossible to tell which Lapoole, Edward or Michael carried out the King's order at the execution of Woodstock, although both were in Calais at that time. Both names are found in Grafton. Edward is given by

Holinshed, Michael by Froissart. But the dramatist's greatest innovation lies in making the intriguing and seditious Woodstock of Froissart an upright man and an innocent victim of Richard's machinations.

> " It was an easy taske to worke on hime:
> His playneness was to open to ther view,
> He feard no wrong, because his harte was trew."

In addition he portrayed Woodstock as continually pacifying Lancaster and York, when the Duke was actually stirring them up to rebellion against Richard. He added an elaborate Masque to Richard's plot for taking Woodstock; and in the murder scene, although he kept the victim's prayer and confession and the implements of the assassination (feather beds and towels) he cut down the number of murderers from four to two and omitted the shriving priest. To heighten the effectiveness of the scene, he added two ghosts and thunder and lightning. Finally he painted the weakness of Richard in broader colors than the chronicles warranted, and added numerous comic scenes of his own creation.

In spite of these divergencies, his indebtedness to Berners' translation, not only for details of characterization, but also for many of his principal scenes, is clearly evident, as the following summary shows:

ACT ONE.
Scene 2. Richard confers special appointments upon his favorites.
Scene 3. Lancaster delegated to pacify the discontented people.
ACT TWO.
Scenes 1 and 2. Appointment of Parliament by the uncles. Details of the Parliament scene, e. g. *the crowning* of Richard (found only in Froissart).
Scene 3. Weeping Scene. Characters of Duchesses of Ireland and of Gloucester.

10

ACT THREE.
  Scene 2.   York and Lancaster influenced by Gloucester.
ACT FOUR.
  Scene 2.   Capture of Gloucester.
ACT FIVE.
  Scene 1.   Murder of Gloucester.
  Scene 2.   Mourning of the Duchess of Gloucester, and her appeal to Lancaster and York for aid.

From this evidence we may conclude that the writer of *Woodstock* must have read, not a very long time before, a number of chronicles of Richard II, certainly Berners, and either Holinshed, or Grafton. The meagre citations from Stow indicate scarcely more than an extremely reminiscent knowledge of the *Annales.* It is hard to see how the chronicles could have been before him at the time of writing, though passages from each one, especially from Berners' Froissart point to this conclusion.

The play however, as has been mentioned, is noteworthy rather for its departures from historical fact and for its daring praise of sedition. Writers of the chronicle plays of this time generally followed their historical sources carefully, and often strove to give fairly truthful presentations. But the author of *Woodstock* probably from some democratic sympathy, garbled his history with the express intention of elevating at the expense of royalty the character of *Woodstock* to the role of popular hero. Such a play shows how the democratic spirit, greatly obscured by the aristocratic temper of the age, nevertheless smoldered in the hearts of the people, and occasionally flamed forth through such spokesmen as the author of *Woodstock.*

CHAPTER VIII

DANIEL'S CIVIL WARS

In 1590, after making the most of a little Oxford training, Samuel Daniel joined the literary coterie headed by
Sir Philip Sidney's sister, Lady Mary Countess of Pembroke. To her kindness and encouragement Daniel makes
frequent grateful reference in the dedications of his literary
works. In the following year, Daniel was engaged as tutor
to William Herbert, Earl of Pembroke, and in the same
year Nashe first introduced Daniel to the reading public by
surreptitiously publishing twenty-seven of his love sonnets.
In defense Daniel issued in 1592 his complete sonnet se-
quence *Delia* to which he added the new *Complaynt of
Rosamund*.

In October 1594, his *First Foure Bookes of the Civle
Wars* were entered for publication on the Stationers' Register, and in the following year appeared the first quarto.
Another quarto adding a Fifth Book was issued in 1599.
Some of the copies of the *first* quarto have added a Fifth
Book, but, as Grosart explains, this was taken from the edition of 1599, and added to the remaining copies of the 1595
quarto prior to the publication of the 1599 quarto. Critics
in ignorance of this fact, and noticing two differing quartos
dated 1595 have repeatedly stated that Daniel made two
issues in that year.[1] The 1601 Folio Edition included a
sixth and seventh book; and the 1609 quarto an eighth book
concluding with the marriage of Edward IV and Lady

[1] R. G. White originated this theory, which is followed in the very
misleading article on Daniel by Lee in the D.N.B.

Grey. The whole was dedicated to the Countess of Pembroke. In his dedication Daniel said that he hoped to continue the *Civil Wars* "unto the glorious Union of Henry 7," and announced his intention of writing a prose History of England. Although he never completed the *Civil Wars*, he did publish successive parts of the prose *History* in 1612 and 1617, the final account extending from the beginning to the death of Edward III.[2] Daniel modestly stated that this prose *History* was merely a "sewing together" of authorities. But he drew not only from the "common authorities," as he puts it, but also from many private manuscripts, as well as the wealth of material supplied by his distinguished friends William Camden and Sir Robert Cotton. Grosart states that Daniel's "margins show that he had the whole available literature of his *History* at his command, and he promised an Appendix of original MS. documents by aid of Sir Robert Cotton, Camden, etc."[3]

Evidence is not wanting to show that Daniel employed as conscientious a method in preparation for the *Civil Wars* of 1594–5. The epic shows very definite traces of consultation of several chronicles. Among those expressly mentioned by the poet are Polydore Vergil, Froissart and Hall. Dr. Albert Probst of Strassburg who made, in 1902, a Quellenstudie of Daniel's Civil Wars, came to the conclusion (pp. 42–45) that Daniel had recourse to Hall, Holinshed, and Stow for the first two books and to Holinshed and Hall for the last six books of the *Civil Wars*. As Probst did not notice Daniel's two references to Froissart,—one in a note on the text of the *Civil Wars*, and one in the preface to the prose *History*, he confined his researches to Hall, Holinshed, Grafton and Stow, conjecturing that since Daniel had cited these authorities in the preface of his prose

[2] See discussion of Daniel's History in Part I, chap. 3.
[3] Grosart IV, xviii.

History 1612–1618, he probably drew upon them for the *Civil Wars* of 1594–5. But Daniel included in this list not only Hall, Holinshed, Grafton and Stow, but also Froissart and a number of other authorities.

These two independent references to the Froissart chronicle are found in Grosart's edition of Daniel as follows:

1. In a note to a variant reading of stanza 60, Book I of the first Quarto of the *Civil Wars* Daniel writes:

"Froissart, Pol. Virg., and Hall deliver it in this sort." (Gro. II, p. 34).

2. Again in the preface of the prose *History* Daniel cites his authorities as follows:

"In the Lives of Edward the First, Edward the Second and Third: *Froissart* and Walsingham with such Collections as by Polydore Virgil, Fabian, Grafton, Hall, Holinshed, Stow and Speed . . . have been made and divulged to the world."

It is doubtful how far we may with safety rely upon this second list of authorities as indicative of Daniel's sources for the *Civil Wars;* but an independent examination of the chronicles justifies Probst's main contentions that Grafton's Chronicle contributed nothing, and that Holinshed and Stow provided some details for the first two books. It is natural to expect, however, that Daniel would draw largely from the elaborate accounts of Froissart for the reign and deposition of Richard II. Froissart's chronicle has not received the attention in this connection that it deserves, since Daniel expressly mentions him in relation to his epic. The following comparison of the *Civil Wars* with the chronicles reveals Daniel's method of treatment. He seems to have relied mainly upon Berners' Froissart, supplemented with Holinshed, and in a few instances with

Stow. To verify details in certain places, he referred also to Vergil and Hall.[4]

Froissart's narrative resembles more closely the first sixty stanzas of Book I, than any other chronicle. Elaborations of the characters of Lancaster, York, and especially Gloucester (Stz. 25–32) bear out this relationship, while the speech of 'Cont. S. Paule' (Stz. 43–49) is an adaptation of Berners' version. Book I, *stanza 25.*

> Of these, John, Duke of Lancaster, was one.
> Too great a Subject groune, for such a State.
> The title of a King, what he had done
> In great exploits his mind did eleuate
> Aboue proportion Kingdomes stand upon:
> Which made him push at what his issue gate.

In this stanza Daniel refers to Froissart's account of Lancaster's exploits in the Spanish kingdom, and his marriage with Constance daughter of King Peter.   (I. 437.)

". . . Sir Guysharde Dangle shewed the duke sayeng thus: Sir, and it like you, ye are to marry, and we knowe wher is a great maryage for you, wherby you and your heyre shal be Kyng of Castell . . . he was well content . . . and he maryd the eldest, called Constance."

> "The other Edmond Langley, whose mild sprite
> Affected quiet and a safe delight."

From Berners II, 643–4:

". . . the duke of Gloucestre, uncle to the Kynge . . . often tymes spake with his brother the duke of York, and drewe hym as moche as he coulde to his opynions, *for he was but a softe prince. . . .*"

For the character of Woodstock (Duke of Gloucester) in *Stanzas 26–32,* cf. selections under the play *Woodstock.*

---

[4] I find that many of the passages quoted by Probst from Stow are also in Holinshed, so that the influence of the former was probably not so great as Probst asserts it to have been.

An influence of the play *Woodstock* upon the *Civil Wars* might be conjectured here; but it is unlikely, unless Daniel witnessed a performance of *Woodstock* in the theatre, since no quartos of the play were issued. Moreover, the play garbles history deliberately, while the *Civil Wars* shows a truth to history based upon a careful reading of several chronicles.

Stanzas 43–49. Count St. Paul heading an Embassy to Richard from Charles of France, advises Richard to dispose of his uncles. Daniel had in mind Berners, II, 687:

" The Kyng of England spared not to shewe therle of saint Powle the state that England stood in, and howe he founde alwayes his uncle the duke of Gloucestre harde and rebell agaynst hym, and shewed hym all thynge $_y{}^t$ he knewe. When theerle of saynt powle herde the kynge say in that wyse he had great maruele therof, and sayde how it ought nat to be suffered, and sayd: syr, if ye suffre this, they wyll dystroy you; it is sayd in France howe the duke of Gloucestre entendeth to nothynge, but to break the peace and to renewe the warre agayne, and that lytell and litell he draweth the hertes of yonge men of the realme to his parte, for they desyre rather warre than peace; so that the anncyent wyse men, if the war beganne to styne, they shulde *nat be herde nor belued, for reason, right, nor iustyce hath no place nor audyence where as yuell reygneth therefore prouyde therefore rather betymes than to late; it were better ye had* theym in daunger than they you. . . ."

Stanzas 59–75 describing the quarrel between Herford and Mowbray (also treated by Shakespeare in Richard II, Act I) as Daniel states,[5] are based upon Froissart. Holinshed's differing version, which Shakespeare used, makes Herford the accuser and Mowbray the defendant. From *stanza 75 to the end of Book I* the influence of Stow and Holinshed become increasingly apparent especially in furnishing names, e. g., Greene, Aumarle, Milford, etc.

[5] Note to Stanza 60 of the first Quarto.

In *Book II* which, like the Froissart chronicle, ends with
the deposition of Richard, Holinshed and Stow continue
supplementary sources as far as stanza 61.   Here Daniel
introduces the episode of Queen Isabel and Richard, which,
deservedly famous as adapted later by Shakespeare, has
generally been considered pure invention.   This episode,
by far the most beautiful passage in the whole epic, is based
upon accounts of the Queen that Daniel found in Froissart.
In brief outline the episode depicts the state of Richard
returning from his fruitless war in Ireland, which has
depleted his forces and left him in the hands of the banished
Bolingbroke unexpectedly returned from France.   Entering by deception Flint Castle, the King's stronghold,
Bolingbroke with his retinue compels Richard to accompany
him to London.   Meanwhile the Queen anxiously awaits
her beloved husband without a suspicion of what has be-
fallen him in Ireland.   She eagerly watches the army approaching and her heart beats for joy when she thinks she
sees her King riding upon a white horse among his glittering troops.   How great her grief when she discovers that
the leader is Henry Bolingbroke!

> *II,* St. 69.
>> " And foorth shee lookes, and notes the formost traine;
>> And grieues to view some there she wisht not there:
>> Seeing the chiefe not come, stayes, lookes againe;
>> And yet she sees not him that should appeare:
>> Then backe she stands, and then desires as faine
>> Againe to looke, to see if hee were neere:
>> At length a glittering troupe farre off she spies,
>> Perceiues the throng, and heares the shouts and cries,

>> *St. 70*
>> Lo, yonder now at length he comes, sayeth shee:
>> Looke, my goode women, where he is in sight:
>> Do you not see him? yonder, that is hee,

Mounted on that white courser, all in white,
There where the thronging troupes of people bee:
I know him by his seat, he sits upright:
Lo, now he bowes: deare Lord, with what sweet grace!
How long haue I longd to behold that face!

St. 71

O what delight my hart takes by mine eye!
I doubt me, when he comes but something neere.
I shall set wide the window: what care I
Who doth see me, so him I may see cleare?
Thus doth false joy delude her wrongfully
(Sweete Lady) in the thing she held so deare,
For neere come, she findes she had mistooke
And him she markt, was Henry Bullingbroke.

Overcome with grief Isabel rushes again to the window
and sees Richard an ignominious prisoner in Bolingbroke's
train being led past toward London. She learns that he is
to be imprisoned in the Tower, and determines to visit and
comfort him.

Stz. 90

" Entring the chamber, where he was alone
(As one whose former fortune was his shame)
Loathing th' obruding eye of any one
That knew him once, and knowes him not the same:
When hauing given expresse command that none
Should presse to him; yet hearing some that came
Turns angerly about his grieued eye:
When, lo, his sweete afflicted Queene he spyes.

St. 91

" Straight cleares his brow; and with a borrowed smile,
What, my deare Queene? o welcome, deare, he sayes;
And (striuing his owne passsion to beguile,
And hide the sorrow which his eye betrayes)
Could speake no more; but wrings her hands, the while:
And then, Sweet Lady; and againe he stayes:

Th' excesse of joy and sorrow both affordes
Affliction none, or but poore niggard wordes.

St. 92

Shee that was come with a resolved hart,
And with a mouth full stor'd, with wordes well chose;
Thinking, This comfort will I first impart
Unto my Lord, and thus my speech dispose:
Then thus Ile say, thus looke, and with this art
Hide mine owne sorrow to relieue his woes;
When being come, all this prov'd nought but winde;
Teares, lookes, and sighes, as only tell her minde.

St. 93

Thus both stood silent and confused so,
Their eyes relating how their heartes did morne:
Both bigge with sorrow, and both great with wo
In labour with what was not to be borne:
This mightie burthen, wher with all they goe,
Dies undeliuered, perishes unborne;
Sorrow makes silence her best Orator,
Where words may made it lesse, not shew it more.
But he, whom longer time had learn'd the art
T'indure affliction, as a usuall touch;
Straines foorth his wordes, and throwes dismay apart,
To rayse up her, whose passions now were such
As quite opprest her overcharged hart.
(Too small a vessel to containe so much)
And cheeres and mones, and fained hopes doth frame,
As if himself beleeu'd, or hop't the same."

With this stanza ends the episode, nor does Daniel allude
to the Queen again. The major part of the incident has
no foundation in history. There is no authority stating
that Isabel and Richard ever met after his capture by
Bolingbroke. Moreover Isabel at that time was eleven
years of age. Daniel recognizing the difficulty fully apologizes for this anachronism in his prefatory address *To the*

Reader, affirming however, the truth of his epic to history in all other respects:

" And if I haue erred somewhat in the draught of the young Q. Isabel (wife of Ric. 2) in not suting her passions to her yeares: I must craue fauor of my credulous Readers; and hope the young Ladies of England (who peradventure will thinke themselves of age sufficient, at 14 yeares to haue a feeling of their own estates) will excuse me in that point. For the rest, setting aside those ornaments, proper to this kinde of writing, I haue faithfully obsuered the Historie."

No portrait of Queen Isabel is given in the English chronicles, and only in Froissart are passages found that refer to her character and life. In several places Froissart dwells upon the charm, beauty and dignity of the child, who was only eight years old when given by her father Charles of France into Richard's keeping.

Ber., II, 625. ". . . they sayde she was but a yonge chylde of eyght yere of age, wherfore they sayd, there could not be in her no great wysdome nor prudence; howbeit, she was indoctryned well ynough and that the lordes founde well whan they sawe her. The Erle Marshall, beyng on his knees, sayde to her, Fayre lady, by the grace of god ye shall be our lady and quene of Englande. Then answered the yonge lady well aduysedly, without counsayle of any other persone: Syr, quod she, and it please god and my lorde my father that I shall be quene of Englande, I shall be glad thereof, for it is shewed me that I shall be then a great lady. Than she toke up the erle Marshall by the hande, and ledde him to the quene her mother, who had great joy of the answere that she had made, so were all the other that herde it. *The maner, countenance and behauoure of this yonge lady pleased greatly the Ambassadours, and they sayd amonge themselfe, that she was lykely to be a lady of hygh honoure and great goodness.*"

P. 763: " and at the same feest the kynge ordayned to go *into Irelande,* to enploy his men in that voyage and so he departed, *and left the Quene with her trayne styll at Wyndsore. . . .*"

From such hints as these in Froissart Daniel may have derived his character of Queen Isabel which Shakespeare later adopted and elaborated.

That he took the description of Bolingbroke's triumphant procession from Froissart is plain for such details as the "glittering troupe," and Bolingbroke on a "white courser, all in white," are found in no English chronicle, but occur in Berners (II. 746). I quote extracts for the whole episode:

"Than therle sayd: Sir, I se none other remedy but to yelde yourselfe as my prisoner; and whan they knowe that ye be my prisoner they wyll do you no hurte." . . . p. 747.

P. 747. ". . . As soone as they had the kynge thus in their handes, they sent notable persones to the yonge quene, who was at Ledes in Kent, and they cal to the lady Coucy, and sayd to her, Madam, make you redy, for ye must depart hens; and at your departyng make no semblent of displeasure before the quene, but saye howe your husband hath sent for you. . . ."

(P. 747.) ". . . As for the state of the quene was so tourned and broken, for there was lefte nouther man, woman, nor chyld of ye nacion of Frace, nor yet of Englande, suche as were in any favor with the kyng; her house was newly furnisshed with ladyes and damoselles, and other offycers and seruantes; *they were changed all, that in no wyse they shuld nat speke of the kynge, nat one to another.*

(P. 747.) "Thus the duke of Lancastre departed fro Chertsay, and rode to Shene and fro, thens . . . they conueyed the Kyng to the towre of London . . .;" (p. 752) . . . and than the duke . . . departed fro Westmynster and rode to the towre of London with a great nombre. . . . Than had they longe cotes with strayte sleeves, furred with mynyner lyke prelates, *with whyte laces hangynge on* their shulders" . . . (p. 753) . . . "And after dyner the duke departed fro the towre to Westmynster, and rode all the way bareheeded, and aboute his necke the lyuery of Fraunce; he was acompanyed with ye prince his sonne, and syxe dukes, syxe erles, and XVIII barons, and in all, knyghtes and squyers a nyne hundred horse: than the kynge had on a shorte cote of clothe of golde, after the maner of Almayne, *and he was mounted on a whyte courser,* and the garter on his left legge."

These passages from Berners remove doubt as to the ultimate source of the Isabel-Richard episode. How skilfully Daniel adapted the Froissart material; how beautifully he moulded with it the imagined tragic meeting of the King and Queen has already been set forth.

The remaining stanzas of Book II (i. e., 95–117) dealing with Richard's deposition, especially the details of his royal garb and the resignation of the crown with his own hand (a detail that Shakespeare makes much of) are also drawn from Berners II, 751–752.

". . . Than Kynge Rycharde was brought into the hall, aparelled lyke a kynge in his robes of estate, his septer in his hande, and his crowne on his heed: than he stode up alone, nat holden nor stayed by no man, and sayde aloude: I haue been kynge of Englande, duke of Acquytany, and lorde of Irelande, about XXII yeres, whiche sygnory, royalty, cepter, crowne, and herytage, I clerely resygne here to my cosyn Henry of Lancastre: and I desyre hym here in this open presence, in entrynge of the same possessyon, to take this septour: and so delyuered it to the duke, who toke it. *Than Kynge Richarde toke the crowne fro his heed with bothe his handes* and set it before hym, and sayd: Fayre cosyn, Henry duke of Lancastre, I gyve and delyuer you this crowne, wherwith I was crowned Kyng of Englande, and therwith all the right therto dependyng. The duke of Lancastre tooke it. . . ."

The chronicle of Froissart comes to a close with the death of Richard II, though the author writes, "howe he dyed, and by what maner I coulde nat tell whan I wrote this cronycle."

With the beginning of the third book of the *Civil Wars*

comes the ascension of Henry IV and the murder of Richard II by Exton, details that the beginning of Hall's chronicle provides.

From this point the accounts of Berners and Stow drop out and Hall and Holinshed become leading sources—for the remaining books of the poem, III–VIII (Cf. Probst, pp. 16–45).

CHAPTER IX

The problem of assigning a date to Shakespeare's *Richard II* involves an interesting discussion of its relation to Daniel's *Civil Wars*. The similarity between the two works often referred to by editors and critics of Shakespeare, was first noted by Knight in his Pictorial edition of the plays. On the evidence of certain parallel passages he came to the conclusion that Shakespeare had read Daniel's epic prior to writing *Richard II*. Later authorities, however, Delius, White, Clark-Wright, Ward, Rolfe, Gollancz, agree in thinking that Daniel and not Shakespeare was the borrower. But the recent discussions of Porter and of Craig show that the trend of opinion is now in the other direction.

Daniel's *First Four Books of the Civil Wars* was entered on the Stationers' Register in October, 1594, and Shakespeare's *Richard II* on the 29th of August, 1597; the former appearing in quarto in 1595, and the latter in 1597. With regard to the year in which Shakespeare wrote the play, two traditions have become firmly established, both of which are unreliable,—one originated by Malone, the other by Richard Grant White. Malone stated that the play was written in 1593, though in former editions of the same essay, he had assigned 1597, dates for which he offered no evidence. Succeeding critics, Delius, Clark-Wright, Ward, Sidney Lee, Gollancz, Dowden and others have accepted Malone's early date and endeavored to establish it by internal evidences of style and rhyme. The other

143

tradition, begun by White, and accepted by Fleay, Rolfe, and others, set 1595 as an absolute date for the play. From a comparison of an original quarto of the *Civil Wars*, to which he had access, with Knight's passages, White concluded that Daniel issued two quartos of the epic in 1595, making certain alterations in the second quarto to agree with Shakespeare's *Richard II*, which had meanwhile appeared. But as Grosart notes, and as Miss Charlotte Porter has further explained,[1] there were not two different quartos of 1595, but only one issue, and assignments of date based on supposition are therefore false.

Knight believing Shakespeare the debtor, held that he wrote *Richard II* after 1595 and shortly before 1597. There seems to be no good reason for disagreeing with Knight's date 1595–7, since all the external evidence harmonizes with this conclusion. The *Civil Wars* appeared in 1595, having been entered on the Stationers' Register in the preceding year, and Shakespeare's *Richard II* appeared both on the Register and in quarto in 1597; hence if Shakespere's play, as all external evidences point, was first acted any time in 1595, it is clear that he borrowed from Daniel. Moreover, it is likely that Daniel's *Civil Wars* was circulated among his friends in manuscript before being placed on the Register in 1594.

The only internal evidences in favor of Malone's conjectural date 1593, are those of style and rhyme; "but rhyme is a conscious element in composition; it may have been due to reaction, or to some passing literary influence. The other metrical tests offer no obstacles to so late an assignment; but are in fact confirmatory. It is to be noted that rhyme militates against the speech-ending test, and that though *Richard II* is not high in feminine endings (11 per

---

[1] First Folio Edition Richard II, Crowell, 1903–10, pp. xv–xvii; 125–6.

cent.) it has a full number of feminine mid-line syllables. It is also true that *Richard II* has a great many verbal conceits, puns, epigrams, and rhetorical figures, things characteristic of Shakespeare's early work. This kind of language is, however, put mainly into the mouths of Richard and of Gaunt, as if with the conscious purpose of characterization."[2] Moreover, there seems to be very good reasons for agreeing with Knight, Craig and others that Shakespeare, and not Daniel was the borrower. It is extremely unlikely that Shakespeare, contemplating his history cycle, should not have read a poem on the same subject written by a recognized poet who was befriended by Southampton; who was engaged as tutor in the Pembroke family, and who was probably his own friend. Although it is a commonplace that Shakespeare followed Holinshed with surprising fidelity,[3] the points in common between the *Civil Wars* and the play, which differ from any known chronicle, are too obvious and numerous to be swept aside as inconsequential, or as mere coincidence. Probst[4] and others have revealed the indebtedness of *Henry IV, 1 and 2* to Daniel's epic, and "*Richard II* bears the same relationship to the *Civil Wars* that *1 and 2 Henry IV* do; the resemblances are of precisely the same sort, and they are quite as close and as numerous."

Of *even more striking effect* than these evidences are the numerous parallels between Daniel and Shakespeare, not only in verbal similarity, but principally in character and in situations for which the English chronicler offers no authority.

[2] For the quotations above I am indebted to the excellent summary by Prof. Hardin Craig, Richard II. Tudor Shakespeare, Macmillan, 1912. (Introd., viii–ix.)

[3] Boswell-Stone: Shakespeare's Holinshed.

[4] Probst, pp. 71–4.

I. Both Shakespeare and Daniel give identical reasons why Richard banished Herford; viz, for fear of Bolingbroke's popularity with the common people.

Daniel, I, St. 63.

> For now considering (as it likely might)
> The victories should hap on Herford's side
> (A man most valiant and of noble sprite,
> Belou'd of all, and euer worthy tri'd)
> How much he might be grac't in publique sight,
> By such an act, as might advance his pride,
> And so become more popular by this;
> Which he feared, too much he already is.
> And therefore he resolues to banish both.

Shakespeare, I, 4, 233 ff

> Ourself and Bushy, Bagot here and Green
> Observed his courtship to the common people:
> How he did seem to dive into their hearts
> With humble and familiar courtesy,
> What reverence he did throw away on slaves,
> Wooing poor craftsmen with the craft of smiles
> And patient underbearing of his fortune,
> As 'twere to banish their affects with him.

Daniel's source for this motive was Berners' II, p. 715:

". . . and, sir, knowe for certayne, that if ye suffre these two Erles to come into the place to do batayle, ye shall not be lorde of the felde, but the Londoners and suche lordes of their parte wyll rule the felde, for the loue and fauoure that they beare to the erle of Derby; and the erle Marshall is soore hated, and specially the Londoners would he were slayne;"

2. Both poets introduce the Queen as a mature woman, who according to the chronicles was eleven years of age. Daniel, as has already been noted, offered an elaborate apology for this anachronism, a fact which certainly goes far as evidence that he was the originator, for what could

be the point of his apology, if Shakespeare had recently preceded him in exhibiting on the stage precisely the same thing? The original of Queen Isabel then is Daniel's adaptation of Froissart, for evidence is yet wanting to prove that Shakespeare had access to Froissart for any one of his chronicle plays. Moreover, Shakespeare's characterization is the enlarged and modified portrait of Daniel's. The drawing is deeper and more subtle. In the *Civil Wars* the Queen appears but once, in *Richard II*, three times; and Shakespeare heightens the portrayal by the noteworthy scene between the Queen and the Gardner. As Miss Porter notes:

" She is made dramatically useful in foreshadowing evil to Richard, vaguely to begin with (II, i); then with a shrewd and bitter particularity[5] (III, iv); finally, the Poet influences through her an increasing sympathy for Richard. . . ." " If Daniel borrowed from Shakespeare here, it was stupid in him not to borrow more, and equivocal, moreover, to apologize for introducing Isabel, as he did, in his Preface without any admission of his indebtedness."[6]

3. The descriptions of the triumphant Bolingbroke leading the despised and neglected Richard captive, through the Londoners, and past Queen Isabel, are strikingly parallel. For this picture, there is no historical source in the English chronicles. In Froissart Bolingbroke leads Richard to London and the Tower in the night to avoid the people. I quote the entire episode as it appears first in Daniel and later in Shakespeare.

Daniel, II, 61 ff.
    Straight towards London in the heate of pride,
    The Duke sets forward as they had decreed

5 Daniel's Queen exhibited sweetness and resignation, and no bitterness.
6 First Folio, pp. xvi–xvii.

With whom, the captive King constrained must ride
Most meanly mounted on a simple steed:
Degraded of all grace and ease beside,
Thereby neglect of all respect to breed
For, th 'ouer-spreading pompe of prouder might
Must darken weakness, and debase his sight.

62.

Approaching neere the Cittie, hee was met
With all the sumptuous shewe joy could devise
Where new-desire to please did not forget
To passe the usuall pompe of former guise
Striuing applause, as out of prison let,
Runnes-on, beyond all bounds to nouelties
And voyce, and hands, and knees, and all do now
A strange deformed forme of welcome showe

63.

And manifold Confusion running greetes,
Shootes, cries, claps hands, thrusts, striues and presses near,
Houses improv'risht were, t'inrich the streetes,
And streetes left naked, that unhappie were
Plac't from the sight where Joy with Wonder meetes;
Where all, of all degrees, striue to appeare;
Where diuers-speaking Zeale one murmure findes,
In vndistinguisht voyce to tell their mindes.

64.

He that in gloire of his fortune date,
Admiring what hee thought could neuer be,
Did feel his blood within salute his state,
And lift vp his reiocying soule, to see
So many hands and hearts congratulate
Th' advancement of his long-desir'd degree;
When, prodigall of thankes, in passing by,
He resalutes them all, with chearefull eye.

65.

Behind him, all aloofe, came pensive on
The unregarded King; that drooping went

Alone, and (but for spight) scarce lookt upon:
Iudge, if hee did more enuie, or lament
See what a wondrous work this day is done
Which th' image of both fortunes doth present:
In th' one, to shew the best of glories face;
In the other, worse than worst of all disgrace."

Richard, II (V, 2).

" *Duch.* At that sad Stoppe my Lord,
Where rude mis-govern'd hands, from Windowes tops,
Threw dust and rubbish on King Richard's head.

Yorke. Then, as I said, the Duke, great Bullingbrooke,
Mounted upon a hot and fierie Steed,
With his aspiring Rider seem'd to know,
With slow, but stately pace, kept on his course:
Whilst all tongues cride, god save thee Bullingbrooke,
You would have thought the very windowes spake,
So many greedy lookes of yong and old,
Through Casements darted their desiring eyes
Upon his visage: and that all the walled,
With painted Imagery had said at once,
Jesus preserve thee, welcom Bullingbrooke.
Whil'st he, from the one side to the other turning,
Bare-headed, lower then his proud Steedes necke,
Bespake them thus: I thanke you Countrimen:
And thus still doing, thus he past along.

Dutch. Alack poore Richard, where rode he the whil'st?

Yorke. As in a Theater, the eyes of men
After a well graced Actor leaves the Stage,
Are idley bent on him that enters next,
Thinking his prattle to be tedious:
Even so, or with more contempt, mens eyes
Did scowle on gentle *Richard;* no man criede, God save him:
No joyfull tongue gave him his welcome home,
But dust was throwne upon his Sacred head,
Which with such gentle sorrow he shooke off.

His face still combating with teares and smiles
That had not god (for some strong purpose) steel'd
(The badges of his greefe and patience)
The hearts of men, they must perforce have melted,
And Barbarisme it selfe have pittied him."

4. After the scene in the streets, both poets portray a tragic meeting between Richard and Isabel:

Act IV

C.W. (II, 66 ff.).
" Now *Isabell*, the young afflicted Queene
(Whose yeares had neuer shew'd her but delights,
Nor louely eyes before had euer seene
Other then smiling ioyes, and ioyfull sights;
Borne great, matcht great, liv'd great, and euer beene
Partaker of the world's best benefits)
Had plac't her selfe, hearing her Lord *should passe*
That way, where she unseene in secret was;
Sick of delay, and longing to behold
Her long-mist Loue . . .
At last, her loue-quick eyes . . .
Fastens on one; whom though she neuer tooke
Could be her Lord; *yet that sad cheere which hee*
Then shew'd, his habit and his woful looke,
The grace he doth in base attire retains:
Caus'd her she could not from his sight refraine.

. . . .

Yet god forbid; let me deceived be,
And be in not my Lord, although it may
Let me not see him, but himselfe; a King:
For so he left me; so he did remoue.
This is not he: this feeles some other Thing."

Rich. II, V:
" This way the King will come; this is the way
To *Julius Caesar's* ill-erected Tower:
To whose flint Bosome, my condemned Lord

Is doomed a Prisoner, by proud *Bullingbroke*
        Enter Richard, and Guard

But softe, but see, or rather doe not see,
My faire Rose wither; yet looke up: behold'
That you in pittie may dissolve to dew,
And wash him fresh againe with true-love Teares,
Ah, thou, the Modell where old Troy did stand,
Thou Mappe of Honor, thou King Richard's Tombe,
And not King Richard. . . ."

5. In both poems Bolingbroke courts the favor of the common people, and his growing power is described by Daniel thus:

C.W. (II, i).
All turn'd their faces to the *rising sunne*
And leaue his setting-fortune *night begunne.*

by Shakespeare:

Richard II (III, 2, 217 ff.):
Discharge my followers; let them hence away,
From Richard's *night* to Bolingbroke's *fair day.*

6. Similar portents in the heavens.

C.W. (I, 113–114):
" Amazing Comets, threatning Monarchs might,
And new-scene *Starres,* unknown unto the night,
Red fiere Dragons in the ayre do flye,
And burning *Meteors,* pointed-streaming lightes:
Bright Starres in midst of day appeare in skie."

Rich. II (II, iv, 9–10):
" And *Meteors* fright the fixed *Starres* of Heaven;
And pale-fac'd Moone lookes bloody on the Earth."

also *C.W.* (I. 118):

" Th'ungodly blood-shed that did so defile
The beautie of thy fields, and euen did marre
The flowre of thy chiefe pride, thou fairest Ile:"

Rich. II (III, iii, 97) :
Ten thousand bloody crownes of Mother's sonnes
Shall ill become the *flower of England's face.*

7. Daniel calls Henry by the familiar name *Bullingbroke*
(I, 8) and spells the title *Herford,* not *Hereford* as in
Holinshed. Shakespeare adopts the same name, and writes
Bullingbroke which is not in Holinshed, and spells *Herford*
after Daniel.

8. In the two deposition scenes, Richard delivers the
crown to Bolingbroke with his own hand.

C.W. (II, 112) from Berners II, p. 752.

" Tis said, with his owne hand he gaue the Crowne "

Rich. II (IV, i, 210) :

"With mine owne Hands I give away my Crowne."

9. After Bolingbroke has ascended the throne, the coun-
ter-plotters to restore Richard swear in both poems by the
Sacrament.

C.W. (III, 35) :
" A solemne oath religiously they take
By intermutuall vowes protesting there,
This neuer to reveale: nor to forsake
So good a Cause, for danger, hope or feare:
The *Sacrament,* the pledge of faith, they take:"

Rich. II (IV, 1, 332–3) :
Abbot. " Before I freely speake my minde herein,
You shall not onely *take the Sacrament.*"

10. Bolingbroke in each case gives identical hints for the
murder of Richard.

C.W. (III, 57) :

" And wisht that some would so his life esteeme,
　As *ridde him of these feares* wherin he stood."

Rich. II (V, iv) :

" Have I no friend will rid me of this living feare."

11. In both versions just before his death Richard engages in a soliloquy comparing and contrasting the state of the King and of a lowly man, cf. *C.W.* (III, 65–69) ; *Rich. II* (V, v) ; and in both a servant rushes in with news from the court, followed instantly by Exton with his murderers.   *C.W.* (III, 70) ; *Rich. II* (V, v, 69 ff.) :

12. Finally Exton is cast off by Bolingbroke for the deed ; nor will the new king assume any responsibility. Shakespeare must have taken this from *C.W.* (III, 78–79) :

" So foule a deed ? where is thy grace in Corte,
　For such a seruice, acted in the sort ?
　First, he for whom thou dost this villanie
　(Though pleas'd therewith) will not avouch thy fact.
　But let the weight of thine owne infamie
　Fall on thee, unsupported, and unbakt : "

Rich II (Last speech in the play)

Bul.　I thank thee not, for thou has wrought
　　　a deed of Slaughter, with thy fatall hand,
　　　Upon my head, and all this famous Land.

Ex.　From your owne mouth my Lord, did I this deed.

Bul.　They love not poyson, that do poyson neede
　　　Nor do I thee, though I did wish him dead.
　　　I hate the murtherer, love him murthered.
　　　The guilt of conscience take thou for thy labour.

With the evidence of these twelve parallels of varying weight and value, *differing from the chronicle sources;* and with the strong external evidence in favor of Daniel's priority and of his consultation of Berners' Froissart, it would seem hazardous and difficult still to maintain that Shakespeare did not have access to the *Civil Wars* shortly before, or while writing *Richard II*. Note should also be taken of the perfect connection between *Richard II* and *Henry IV*, Part I; the former ending and the latter beginning with mention of the expedition to the Holy Land. There seems little reason, then, why *Richard II* should be assigned to a date prior to 1595. The close relation of many scenes to the later plays of the chronicle group, and "the perfect harmony with them in underlying ideas" seems to show that the play was written not four years before its publication, but shortly before its appearance in the Quarto of 1597. If such is the case, Shakespeare, beginning with Richard's life where the anonymous author of *Woodstock* had left it, employed the *Chronicles* of Holinshed and the *Civil Wars* of Daniel for his *Tragedy of Richard II*, drawing from Daniel what Daniel had derived from Froissart and elaborated.

DANIEL, SHAKESPEARE AND DRAYTON

No writer of the period was a greater imitator of preceding literary successes than Michael Drayton (unless it be Shakespeare). The conception of his *Shepherd's Garland* he derived from Spenser's *Shepherd's Calendar;* his *Endimion and Phoebe* from Marlowe's *Hero and Leander;* his *Legend of Piers Gaveston* (1593–4) and his *Barons' Wars* (1596) from Marlowe's *Edward II*. Drayton issued the *Barons' Wars* to rival Daniel's *Civil Wars*, since he deemed that his contemporary was "too much historian in verse." The poem dealing principally with the troublesome reign of Edward II, enters our period of discussion

with the last years of Edward II and the early years of
Edward III, both of which Froissart briefly narrates in
the first chapters of his Chronicle. Dr. Probst, who has
made a careful comparison of the chronicles of Fabian,
Vergil, Holinshed and Froissart with reference to Drayton's epic, has demonstrated that the poet followed Holinshed closely with perhaps a consultation now and then of
Fabian; but with no reference to Vergil and Froissart.
Concerning Froissart, Probst states (pp. 62–63):

" Die französische Chronik von Jean Froissart bot auch in ihren
später ausserordentlich ausführlichen Berichten unserem Dichter
für die Zeit, welche er in seinem Epos behandelte, eigentlich gar
nichts. Das Interesse des französischen Chronisten is weit mehr
auf die Geschichte seines Vaterlandes und auf die Vorgänge in
Frankreich gerichtet, als auf das, was sich in England ereignet
hat wovon er in den meisten Fällen nicht einmal genaue Kenntnis
hat. Er beginnt überhaupt erst dann ausführlicher zu erzählen,
als eine innigere Berührung englischer und französischer Verhält-
nisse dadurch stattfand, dass ein französischer Edelmann eingriff
in die Geschicke des englischen Könighauses, als Hainault mit
seinen Truppen die Königin Isabella unterstützte, den englischen
Thron für sich und den jungen Prinzen von Wales weider zu
gewinnen. Aber auch dann konnten die Ausführungen des französischen Chronisten für den englischen Dichter keine grosse Be-
deutung erlangen, denn bei dem ganzen Berichte des Franzosen
über die letzten Regierungsjahre Edward's II. und die ersten Jahre
Edward's III. hat dieser in erster Linie die Geschicke Hainault's
und seiner französischen Truppen im Auge."

Probst also shows the strong influence that Marlowe's
Edward II exerted upon the *Barons' Wars*,—principally
in the conception of the character of Mortimer (pp. 84 ff.).

The last version of the triumph of Bolingbroke, the consequent disgrace of King Richard, and his tragic meeting
with Queen Isabel was given to Elizabethan literature by

Michael Drayton who probably wrote in emulation of his rivals Daniel and Shakespeare. On October 12, 1597, Drayton's *England's Heroicall Epistles* was entered upon the Stationers' Register. This work contains two farewell epistles from Queen Isabel to Richard and from Richard to Queen Isabel, briefly rehearsing in smooth couplets with fine lyrical and elegiac feeling, the same episode that Daniel had conceived and Shakespeare had elaborated.

A comparison of Drayton's epistles with the *Civil Wars* and *Richard II* would seem to show that although Drayton knew Daniel's episode, he chose to follow Shakespeare's enlarged version, which had been entered upon the Stationers Register only a month and a half before on the twenty-ninth of August. Practically in all respects these two epistles resemble Shakespeare's details, even to the extent of spelling the proper names identically as Shakespeare had done before him; nor would the prose *Notes of the Chronicle history*, which Drayton added after each epistle, indicate that he had made careful consultation of chronicle sources after the more conscientious method of Daniel.

Thus the chronicle of Froissart through the medium of Berners' translation contributed greatly to the story of Richard II, as portrayed by Elizabethan poets and dramatists. By way of Grafton's chronicle the translation furnished the plot of the play *Jack Straw*, and gave directly to *Woodstock* the character of its protagonist as well as other characters and principal scenes. It likewise furnished Samuel Daniel with much of his story in the first books of the *Civil Wars* and gave him hints for his fanciful episode of Richard and Queen Isabel and the triumphant procession of Bolingbroke. Finally Shakespeare derived that part of *Richard II* which he did not take from Holins-hed, from Berners' Froissart as it came through the medium of Daniel's *Civil Wars;* and Drayton in turn followed Shakespeare's version of the same story for two of his *England's Heroicall Epistles.*[7]

[7] It is probable that *The Conquest of Spain by John of Gaunt* entered S.R. 1594, and listed in Henslowe's Diary, was also derived from Berners' Froissart, whose account of the expedition covers over four folio pages; while the English Chronicles devote summary paragraphs.

BIBLIOGRAPHY

The following bibliography includes the principal works referred to in the course of the present study. References of less importance in the text or footnotes have not, as a rule, been included.

Bel, Jehan le: Les Vrayes Chroniques de Messire Jehan le Bel. M. Polain. 2 vols. Bruxelles, 1863.

Berners, Lord: The Chronicles of Froissart. Reprint of Pynson's Edition. 2 vols. London, 1812.

Berners: The Chronicles of Froissart. Edited by W. P. Ker. 6 vols. London, 1901–3.

Berners: The Chronicles of Froissart. G. C. Macaulay. Oxford, 1908.

Boswell-Stone: Shakspere's Holinshed. London, 1907.

Brewer, J. S.: Letters and Papers of Henry VIII. Vols. I–VIII. London, 1862.

Brooke, C. F. Tucker: Shakespeare Apocrypha. Oxford, 1908.

Capell, E.: Prolusions or Select Pieces of Ancient Poetry. London, 1760.

Chandos the Herald: The Black Prince. Coxe, H. C. Roxburgh Club. London, 1842.

Child, F. J.: English and Scottish Popular Ballads.

Churchill, G. B.: Richard III up to Shakespeare. Palaestra X. Berlin, 1900.

Craig, H.: Richard II, Tudor Shakespeare. New York, 1912.

Daniel, S.: Complete Works. Grosart. 5 vols. 1885–1896.

Drayton, M.: Poems. Spenser Society. 1888.

Fabian, R.: New Chronicles of England and France. Reprint of Pynson edition. London, 1811.

158

Fleay, F. G.: A Chronicle History of the Life and Work
of William Shakespeare, Player, Poet and Playmaker.
New York, 1886.

Froissart, J.: Chronicles. T. Johnes. 2 vols. London,
1844.

Froissart, J.: Chroniques de J. Froissart. Siméon Luce.
Paris, 1869.

Froissart: Oeuvres de Froissart; M. le baron Kervyn de
Lettenhove. 28 vols. Bruxelles, 1870.

Froissart, J.: Mary Darmsteter. Paris, 1894.

Gairdner, J.: Early Chroniclers of Europe. London.

Grafton, R.: Chronicles. Reprint of 1569 Edition. 2
vols. London, 1809.

Hall, E.: Chronicle. Collated and reprinted; Ellis. London, 1809.

Keller, W.: A Tragedy of Richard II. Shakespeare Jahrbuch XXXV, 1899.

Henslowe, P.: Diary; W. W. Greg. London, 1904.

Heywood, T.: An Apology for Actors. Shakespeare Society Publications. London, 1841–3.

Holinshed, R.: Chronicles of England, Scotland and Ireland. 3 vols. in 2. London, 1587.

Jusserand, J. J.: A Literary History of the English People.
3 vols. New York, 1895–1909.

Kingsford, C.: English Historical Literature in the Fifteenth Century. Oxford, 1913.

Kingsford, C.: Survey of London; John Stow. 2 vols.
Oxford, 1908.

Kittredge, G. L.: Englische Studien XXVI.

Knight, C.: Pictorial Edition of Shakespeare.

Kyd, T.: The Works of Thomas Kyd; F. S. Boas. Oxford, 1901.

Lee, S.: Huon of Bordeaux. Early Eng. Text Society.
2 vols.

Liebau, G.: "König Eduard III von England und die Gräfin von Salisbury": Litterarhistorische Forschungen, Heft XIII. Berlin, 1900.

Liebau, G.: "König Edward III von England im Lichte europaischer Poesie," Anglistische Forschungen. Heidelburg, 1901.

Lowes, J. L.: Prologue to the Legend of Good Women, as related to the French Marguerite Poems. Publications of the Modern Language Association. Vol. XIX.

Mirror for Magistrates: Haselwood. 3 vols. London, 1815.

Nash, T.: Works. Mckerrow, R. B. 5 vols. London, 1904.

Painter, W.: Palace of Pleasure; Joseph Jacobs. 3 vols. London, 1890.

Porter, C.: Richard II. First Folio edition. New York, 1903.

Probst, A.: Samuel Daniel's Civil Wars . . . und Michael Drayton's Barons' Wars. Eine Quellenstudie. Strassburg, 1902.

Schütt: The Life and Death of Jack Straw. Kiel, 1901.

Schelling, F. E.: English Chronicle Play. New York, 1908.

Smith, G. G.: Elizabethan Critical Essays. 2 vols. Oxford, 1904.

Smith, R. M.: Edward III. The Journal of English and Germanic Philology. 1911.

Speed, J.: History of Great Britaine. London, 1611.

Spingarn, J. E.: Critical Essays of the Seventeenth Century. 3 vols. Oxford, 1908–9.

Stow, J.: Annales. London, 1631.

Thorndike, A. H.: Tragedy. Boston, 1908.

Ward, A. W.: A History of English Dramatic Literature. 3 vols. London, 1899.

Warnke and Proescholdt: Pseudo-Shakespearian Plays. Halle, 1886.

INDEX

161

This Monograph has been approved by the Department of English and Comparative Literature in Columbia University as a contribution to knowledge worthy of publication.

A. H. THORNDIKE,

Executive Officer